Electronic Resources: Use and User Behavior

Electronic Resources: Use and User Behavior has been co-published simultaneously as *The Reference Librarian*, Number 60 1998.

Forthcoming topics in *The Reference Librarian* series:

• The Holocaust: Memories, Research, Reference, Numbers 61/62

Published:

Electronic Resources: Use and User Behavior has been co-published simultaneously as *The Reference Librarian*, Number 60 1998.

The Haworth Press, Inc., 10 Alice Street, Binghamton, NY 13904-1580 USA

Cover design by Thomas J. Mayshock Jr.

Library of Congress Cataloging-in-Publication Data

Electronic resources : use and user behavior / Hemalata Iyer, editor.
     p. cm.
    Also published as The reference librarian, no. 60, 1998
    Includes bibliographical references and index.
    ISBN 0-7890-0372-4 (acid-free paper)
    1. Electronic information resources–United States. 2. Computer network resources–United States. 3. Academic libraries–United States–Reference services. I. Iyer, Hemalata. II. Reference librarian.
ZA4060.E44 1998
025.04–dc21
                                                 97-49184
                                                  CIP

Electronic Resources: Use and User Behavior

Hemalata Iyer
Editor

Electronic Resources: Use and User Behavior has been co-published simultaneously as *The Reference Librarian*, Number 60 1998.

The Haworth Press, Inc.
New York · London

INDEXING & ABSTRACTING

Contributions to this publication are selectively indexed or abstracted in print, electronic, online, or CD-ROM version(s) of the reference tools and information services listed below. This list is current as of the copyright date of this publication. See the end of this section for additional notes.

- *Academic Abstracts/CD-ROM,* EBSCO Publishing Editorial Department, P.O. Box 590, Ipswich, MA 01938-0590

- *Academic Search: data base of 2,000 selected academic serials, updated monthly:* EBSCO Publishing, 83 Pine Street, Peabody, MA 01960

- *CNPIEC Reference Guide: Chinese National Directory of Foreign Periodicals,* P.O. Box 88, Beijing, People's Republic of China

- *Current Awareness Abstracts,* Association for Information Management, Information House, 20-24 Old Street, London EC1V 9AP, England

- *Current Index to Journals in Education,* Syracuse University, 4-194 Center for Science and Technology, Syracuse, NY 13244-4100

- *Educational Administration Abstracts (EAA),* Sage Publications, Inc., 2455 Teller Road, Newbury Park, CA 91320

- *IBZ International Bibliography of Periodical Literature,* Zeller Verlag GmbH & Co., P.O.B. 1949, d-49009 Osnabruck, Germany

- *Index to Periodical Articles Related to Law,* University of Texas, 727 East 26th Street, Austin, TX 78705

- *Information Science Abstracts,* Plenum Publishing Company, 233 Spring Street, New York, NY 10013-1578

- *Informed Librarian, The,* Infosources Publishing, 140 Norma Road, Teaneck, NJ 07666

- *INSPEC Information Services,* Institution of Electrical Engineers, Michael Faraday House, Six Hills Way, Stevenage, Herts SG1 2AY, England

(continued)

- *INTERNET ACCESS (& additional networks) Bulletin Board for Libraries ("BUBL") coverage of information resources on INTERNET, JANET, and other networks.*
  - <URL:http://bubl.ac.uk/>
  - The new locations will be found under <URL:http://bubl.ac.uk/link/>.
  - Any existing BUBL users who have problems finding information on the new service should contact the BUBL help line by sending e-mail to <bubl@bubl.ac.uk>.
  The Andersonian Library, Curran Building, 101 St. James Road, Glasgow G4 0NS, Scotland

- *Journal of Academic Librarianship: Guide to Professional Literature, The,* Grad School of Library & Information Science/Simmons College, 300 The Fenway, Boston, MA 02115-5898

- *Konyvtari Figyelo-Library Review,* National Szechenyi Library, Centre for Library and Information Science, H-1827 Budapest, Hungary

- *Library & Information Science Abstracts (LISA),* Bowker-Saur Limited, Maypole House, Maypole Road, East Grinstead, West Sussex, RH19 1HH England

- *Library Literature,* The H.W. Wilson Company, 950 University Avenue, Bronx, NY 10452

- *MasterFILE: updated database from EBSCO Publishing,* EBSCO Publishing, 83 Pine Street, Peabody, MA 01960

- *Newsletter of Library and Information Services,* China Sci-Tech Book Review, Library of Academia Sinica, 8 Kexueyuan Nanlu, Zhongguancun, Beijing 100080, People's Republic of China

- *OT BibSys,* American Occupational Therapy Foundation, P.O. Box 31220, Bethesda, MD 20824-1220

- *Referativnyi Zhurnal (Abstracts Journal of the All-Russian Institute of Scientific and Technical Information,* 20 Usievich Street, Moscow 125219, Russia

- *Sage Public Administration Abstracts (SPAA),* Sage Publications, Inc., 2455 Teller Road, Newbury Park, CA 91320

(continued)

SPECIAL BIBLIOGRAPHIC NOTES

related to special journal issues (separates)
and indexing/abstracting

☐ indexing/abstracting services in this list will also cover material in any "separate" that is co-published simultaneously with Haworth's special thematic journal issue or DocuSerial. Indexing/abstracting usually covers material at the article/chapter level.

☐ monographic co-editions are intended for either non-subscribers or libraries which intend to purchase a second copy for their circulating collections.

☐ monographic co-editions are reported to all jobbers/wholesalers/approval plans. The source journal is listed as the "series" to assist the prevention of duplicate purchasing in the same manner utilized for books-in-series.

☐ to facilitate user/access services all indexing/abstracting services are encouraged to utilize the co-indexing entry note indicated at the bottom of the first page of each article/chapter/contribution.

☐ this is intended to assist a library user of any reference tool (whether print, electronic, online, or CD-ROM) to locate the monographic version if the library has purchased this version but not a subscription to the source journal.

☐ individual articles/chapters in any Haworth publication are also available through the Haworth Document Delivery Service (HDDS).

Electronic Resources: Use and User Behavior

CONTENTS

MANAGING ELECTRONIC RESOURCES

ABOUT THE EDITOR

Hemalata Iyer, PhD, is Associate Professor at the University at Albany, State University of New York, where she teaches courses at the Master's level. She also teaches in the Doctoral program in Information Science. Her academic interests focus on information organization within the larger context of information retrieval. She is the author of several articles on classification and indexing, focusing on methods of structuring and representing information. Her book *Classificatory Structures: Concepts, Relations and Representations* examines knowledge structures from a variety of disciplinary perspectives. In addition to her teaching and research, Dr. Iyer serves as the U.S. Regional Coordinator for the International Society for Knowledge Organization.

Introduction

The new technologies have facilitated improved access to information and accelerated the speed of information transfer. As a result, libraries and information centers are faced with the challenges of managing the new electronic resources and assisting library patrons with using them. While CD-ROMs and online search services have been available for several years, patron access to the Internet and Geographic Information Systems (GIS) resources are the newest services provided by libraries. Electronic access has made the task of the reference librarian even more complex, since users tend to expect instant satisfaction of their information needs. In addition to these rising user expectations, the librarian has also to become teacher and trainer.

This volume is devoted to electronic resources and their use in libraries. The main emphasis is on the newer resources, namely the Internet and the GIS. The topics covered in this collection range from theoretical models of user interaction, to their actual searching behavior, and to the management of electronic resources.

Ruth A. Palmquist and Kyung-Sun Kim present some theories relating to information system use and users. The articles by Ingrid Hsieh-Yee, Ruth A. Palmquist and Susan P. Sokoll focus on the Internet resources. Lixin Yu gives an overview of the GIS and their use in libraries. Virginia A. Papandrea and Jane M. Subramanian address the management of electronic resources.

Hemalata Iyer

[Haworth co-indexing entry note]: "Introduction." Iyer, Hemalata. Co-published simultaneously in *The Reference Librarian* (The Haworth Press, Inc.) No. 60, 1998, p. 1; and: *Electronic Resources: Use and User Behavior* (ed: Hemalata Iyer) The Haworth Press, Inc., 1998, p. 1. Single or multiple copies of this article are available for a fee from The Haworth Document Delivery Service [1-800-342-9678, 9:00 a.m. - 5:00 p.m. (EST). E-mail address: getinfo@haworth.com].

USE AND USERS:
SOME THEORIES

Modeling the Users
of Information Systems:
Some Theories and Methods

Ruth A. Palmquist
Kyung-Sun Kim

SUMMARY. Understanding user needs and the ways in which users utilize information systems is important since it can help us in developing and designing more effective and efficient information systems. This paper examines some of the theories that have evolved to explain what kind of mental processes are required for the use of information systems. Research on users of information systems is categorized into two basic groups (system-oriented vs. user-oriented studies), and reviewed. A sample of methodologies used for examining users and their information seeking behavior is then introduced

Ruth A. Palmquist is Assistant Professor, and Kyung-Sun Kim is a doctoral candidate, both at the Graduate School of Library and Information Science, The University of Texas, SZB 564 D7000, Austin, TX 78712.

[Haworth co-indexing entry note]: "Modeling the Users of Information Systems: Some Theories and Methods." Palmquist, Ruth A., and Kyung-Sun Kim. Co-published simultaneously in *The Reference Librarian* (The Haworth Press, Inc.) No. 60, 1998, pp. 3-25; and: *Electronic Resources: Use and User Behavior* (ed: Hemalata Iyer) The Haworth Press, Inc., 1998, pp. 3-25. Single or multiple copies of this article are available for a fee from The Haworth Document Delivery Service [1-800-342-9678, 9:00 a.m. - 5:00 p.m. (EST). E-mail address: getinfo@haworth.com].

and described. Finally, implications of these theories and methods for librarians and information specialists are discussed. *[Article copies available for a fee from The Haworth Document Delivery Service: 1-800- 342-9678. E-mail address: getinfo@haworth.com]*

INTRODUCTION

In everyday life, we often find ourselves needing information to answer questions posed by ourselves as well as others. Although we sometimes do not know exactly what information we want, we still try to locate and use sources that seem to be capable of providing the information that is "wanted." For this, we often ask for help from other people like librarians, search for the information in places like libraries or take advantage of other available information resources and systems.

With the advent of computer technology, more information databases have become available in machine-readable formats and many information systems have been developed and designed for facilitating information retrieval. Ideally, information systems should make the information search so easy that most information searchers need less and in some cases no human assistance. Since the systems are not as responsive or as flexible as human helpers might be, users are doubly burdened when searching for the information they need. Users must not only figure out what they really want to know but also understand how the system should be used.

As information systems are developed based on different technologies and for different purposes, their ways of functioning vary from one to another. This implies that each system might require the user to be equipped with different psychological and/or physical skills in order to get the best result from the system.

How do individuals use an information system? What kinds of factors affect users' interaction with a system? There are a variety of potential variables, but users' psychological aspects, especially cognitive aspects, have been viewed as some of the more important factors influencing human-computer interaction. These cognitive factors have been investigated for the last 10 to 15 years in numerous studies, and it is not our intent to review them all here. However, the focus of this issue brought together some discussion of the more prominent theories in use presently and seemed to require some description of applicable methodologies that can be applied to further our professional understanding of users' computer interaction behaviors.

In this paper, human cognitive aspects related to the use of information systems will be a primary focus. The guiding definition of human cognition for our purposes has been defined fairly simplistically as–behavior displayed which stems from what the user thinks or knows. The word "cognitive" has been much used in our literature and in other disciplines as well. But the emphasis here remains upon the users' ability to think, learn, and problem-solve using various information systems, and the ability for the library and information science (LIS) field to better understand that interaction. Following a discussion of some of the recent work of developing cognitive models of the user, we will present a discussion of research methodologies that seem useful in examining these human cognitive features of users. Finally, the role of reference librarians in working with users and systems will be discussed.

USE OF INFORMATION SYSTEMS

Why Do We Use an Information System?

When individuals have an information need or find a gap between their existing knowledge and a new situation, they select an information system and use it in order to find that which seems needed to fulfill the information need or fill in the perceived gap. The system may be an informal one like asking a friend or relative, or a formal one like using a library.

Selecting an information system is influenced by many factors including psychological, social, economic, and cultural factors. Individuals' perceptions of, experiences with, and expectations of a system, the availability and the characteristics of a system are some examples of such factors. The use made of an information system is also affected by those factors. The interactions of user's psychological perceptions and various systems' characteristics seem particularly important since they affect the ways of using a system more directly than others.

Cognitive Aspects Related to the Use of an Information System

Using an information system seems to require three different cognitive processes: (1) information-seeking, (2) knowledge acquisition and (3) problem solving. Information seeking is a goal-driven activity in which needs are satisfied through problem-solving (Brown, 1991). According to Krikelas (1983), information-seeking behavior begins with a "perceived need," which is much like Belkin's (1980) "anomalous state of knowledge (ASK)," or what Taylor (1968) identified as "a vague dissatisfaction." However described, the gap is caused by something which is strong enough to move the individual to address the perceived inadequacy of an existing understanding and to move the individual, in the case of a library visit, to some new situation in which to better address the perceived inadequacy. The information-seeking behavior required involves those activities that will satisfy the need. When the need (or gap) is no longer perceived, the individual quits the chosen information-seeking process. The process is dynamic since methods of collecting information can vary in time and depend on the immediacy of results (Krikelas, 1983; Rouse, 1984). The ways of collecting and selecting information are also related to the personal habits of the searcher and can also be influenced by the kind of needs to be satisfied.

Knowledge acquisition is what one might normally call "learning." Conceptually, learning is the reorganization of knowledge structures. Through the learning process, an individual restructures the knowledge, organized by others, in order to make it fit in his/her own knowledge structure. While using an information system, individuals get to reorganize their knowledge structure based on either accidentally or intentionally retrieved new information. This ability of information to create structural change was argued by Belkin and Robertson (1976) to be the primary phenomenon of this LIS (Library and Information Science) field, but it has been a difficult phenomenon to fully understand and document.

Problem-solving is another cognitive process required for using a system. Problem-solving starts with a perceived problem. Once the problem is stated in terms that can be understood, individuals then apply their knowledge to the problem and attempt to try out possible solutions. When using an information system, individuals develop strategies that they believe will help to get the best result from the system. System users have to figure out how a system works, how to get a wanted result from the system, how to select the "best" result from the retrieved information, etc.

The key to the effective use of systems seems far from trivial. It depends upon the ability to orchestrate all of the aforementioned cognitive processes, and the ability to do that varies according to a variety of cognitive styles. Cognitive styles are defined as the characteristic ways in which an individual organizes and processes information (Goldstein & Blackman, 1978), and cognitive style has been shown to influence the manner in which individuals prefer to learn and receive instructions (Messick, 1976). Cognitive styles are usually described using different dimensions. Martens (1979) provides a detailed identification of many of the dimensions currently discussed in cognitive theory including field dependence/independence, breadth of categorizing, conceptualizing styles, cognitive complexity/simplicity, constructed/flexible control, and so on.

RESEARCH ON INFORMATION SYSTEM USERS

The development of computer technologies has provided a strong physical and conceptual mechanism for assisting information-seeking activities. Online database systems have been developed to help users retrieve desired information more quickly than can be accomplished from printed ones, for example. Many users, however, express difficulty when using these online systems. The need to minimize the difficulties that the user experiences with a system and maximize the effectiveness and the efficiency of their use has never been greater. Central to our ability to do so rests the cognitive theories that try to help intermediaries and systems designers anticipate the behavior of users.

Cognitive Model and User Model

Understanding what a system can do and what the users of a system expect from it can be facilitated by cognitive modeling. Cognitive modeling also helps system designers develop systems that users can more easily understand because they can anticipate what users require to manipulate the system more effectively.

According to Daniels (1986), cognitive models refer to "images that the components of a system have of themselves, of each other, and of the world." Their focus is not only on cognitive representations of objects but also on the cognitive processes related to these constructed images. These cognitive models "enable individuals to make inferences and predictions, to understand phenomena, to decide what action to take, and to control its [the actions] execution, and above all to experience events by proxy" (Johnson-Laird, 1983).

Cognitive models found in the LIS literature generally consist of three different types: conceptual, mental and user models. According to Borgman (1984), a conceptual model is "a model of the system as the designer wants the user to envision the system" whereas a mental model is "a model that the user builds in his or her head" as he or she interacts with a system. A user model is a third type of cognitive model that Rich (1983) defines as "a model of users interacting with complex systems." Information of situations and tasks as well as more detailed information about groups of users can also be encoded in these models, the hope being that they will be more predictive of the success that will be achieved if more effective interfaces are developed. Various types of user models have been considered important in many research areas varying from education to software engineering.

There are additional ways of classifying user models. Quantitative vs.

analytical models, process vs. non-process models, and dynamic vs. static models are just some examples. According to Carbonell (1986), quantitative models are "abstract formalizations of a general class of users defined in terms of the design parameters of a user interface." For establishing this kind of user model, data from the "average" person's performance in various environments can be collected and used. Analytical models attempt to analyze and model a user's cognitive behavior and process the data in a qualitative way. The analytical models are often used to explain the user's cognitive processes on existing systems or to anticipate the user's reaction toward a new system, whereas quantitative models can only show the user's reactions as they have already occurred on an existing system.

Dynamic and static modeling has been identified by Sparck Jones (1984). Daniels (1986) continues to describe a dynamic model as a model reflecting "changes of state dependent on interaction with the system," and a static model as a model "embodying permanent states of the users." Static models represent permanent features of users, independent of a system's operation, features such as user's gender, domain of knowledge and so on. Dynamic models, in contrast, are concerned with user factors related to the system used, including users' goals and beliefs within a specific context of the system's operation.

Sleeman (1985) views user models as either process or non-process models. Process user models refer to a model focusing on users' structuring process as their mind responds to the outside environment. Non-process user models are those focusing on external variables like tasks to be performed.

These user model classification schemes provide us with a framework for categorizing and assessing different approaches to user studies. In addition, these are closely related to Dervin and Nilan's (1986) distinction between system-oriented and user-oriented approaches in discussion of the progress in user studies.

System-Oriented Studies

In a literature review on information needs and uses, Dervin and Nilan (1986) identified and contrasted two different paradigms applied to user studies: system-oriented and user-oriented approaches. In studies with a system-oriented approach, users are viewed as passive receivers of information, and users' external behavior is observed as an isolated situation. These studies assume that user behavior would stay the same across time and space. Variables with which system-oriented studies are concerned are often demographic information on users (age, gender, etc.), social affiliations (to what group/class does the user belong) and life styles of users, tasks to be performed, etc. The system-oriented approach shares similar views with quantitative, non-process and static user models.

Most user studies, at least among those dated before 1986 when Dervin and Nilan's review appeared, were based on a system-oriented approach. The Cranfield studies in the 1960s and many other IR (Information Retrieval) studies were concerned with the performance evaluation of IR systems by measuring "recall and precision." These studies were done based on an assumption that the average user would be interested in retrieving large amounts of relevant material. The relevance of items retrieved in the Cranfield studies were determined by content experts and believed to represent relevance no matter who the user was. In looking at the performance of a retrieval system, the Cranfield studies represent some of the most system-centered studies in IR.

OPAC (Online Public Access Catalog) user studies in the early 1980s, supported by CLR (Council on Library Resource), are another, but much more moderate, case of system-centered studies. The research was conducted for identifying demographic information about users and nonusers of OPACs, the users' satisfaction, preference, problems that users encounter, etc., by using survey, interview and transaction log analysis methods (Markey, 1984; Matthews, 1983). Although this research attempted to understand more about users, it still had more characteristics of system-oriented studies. Users were viewed as passive reactors to system features, studying variables that were external-to-the-user characteristics like interface features and tasks rather than on variables that were internal-to-the-user characteristics like the user's mental processes.

User-Oriented Studies

User-oriented studies generally view humans as constructive, active users of information and often recognize their psychological as well as societal role in using systems. According to Dervin and Nilan (1986), user-oriented studies are concerned with the more subjective values of information—the values that are perceived by the user. In user-oriented studies, the user is recognized to be in a dynamically changing situation and is held to be moving through the information problematic situation in a way that requires the artifacts of such movement to be interpretation from a more holistic and less reductionistic viewpoint.

Sugar (1995), in a similar review of user-oriented studies, divided recent research efforts into two basic groups: (1) studies with a cognitive approach and (2) studies with a holistic approach. The former is concerned with a user's cognitive aspects while the latter is framed around a user's affective (emotional), psychomotor (physical) characteristics as well as socio-cultural aspects.

Some Cognitive User-Oriented Studies

In system evaluation studies, it is often found that there exist individual differences among users' performance in and reaction to a system, which implies the effect of users' characteristics on user-system interaction. This has led a number of researchers to investigate the relation between human-computer interaction and a user's characteristics, especially those related to cognitive processes.

Spatial visualization ability is a cognitive ability used by an individual to map where he or she is located in a three-dimensional space. Campagnoni and Ehrlich (1989) conducted a research project to investigate the relation between users' spatial visualization ability and their performance in a hypertext system. In their study, participants were given a standard test of spatial visualization ability. They were also asked to find answers to given questions, using a hypertext-based help system. Individuals with good spatial visualization abilities retrieved information faster than those with poor spatial visualization abilities. Apparently, individuals with a good spatial visualization ability were better able to construct a map for the structure of the information space, which helps them save time in finding information in a hypertext system. Campagnoni and Ehrlich also found that the degree of experience with computers affected the ways users had of information-seeking. Users with prior computer knowledge and experience searched information more analytically, exploiting various system features, whereas those with no prior computer experience or knowledge searched in a less systematic manner, essentially "browsing" large displays rather than using system features to minimize retrieved sets.

A user's domain knowledge is another factor that can influence human-computer interaction. In order to examine how "expertise in a subject area" and "expertise in information searching" affect the process and the outcome of information seeking in a hypertext system, Marchionini et al. (1990) conducted an experiment. Participants were divided into three groups according to their level of expertise: (1) a group of novices, (2) a group of experts in a subject and (3) a group of experts in information searching. They were all asked to retrieve information on a given subject in a hypertext system. Both expert groups (subject and search specialists) retrieved information better than the novice group; the subject and search specialists also found more pertinent information and did so more quickly than the novices. Interestingly, no significant difference in the task performance was reported between the two expert groups.

Field-dependence/independence is often studied as influential cognitive style. Identified and intensively studied by Witkin (1978), field-dependence and field-independence refer to an analytical versus a global way of perceiving and both are strongly related to "articulated vs. global cognitive style" (Messick, 1970).

In a study, Korthauer and Koubek (1994) evaluated the effects of an individual's cognitive style on the use of a hypertext system. Initially, participants were divided into two groups based on the level of domain knowledge each participant had about a subject: a group of experts (the experienced) was formed and a group of novices (the naïve). The two main groups were divided again into four subgroups based upon their cognitive style—"field-dependence/independence." The four groups of participants were: (1) field-independent experienced, (2) field-dependent experienced, (3) field-independent naïve, and (4) field-dependent naïve. Each group of participants were asked to answer questions on a topic under two different conditions: an explicit and an inherent condition. Under both conditions, participants were asked questions on a topic. Under the explicit condition, a summary of the given topic was provided. Under the inherent condition no summary was provided. Experienced, field-independent participants performed better at using the hypertext system than experienced, field-dependent participants, especially when questions were asked under the explicit condition. The results suggest an existence of complex interrelationships among knowledge structures and cognitive styles of users and task types when using a hypertext system.

Ellis, Ford and Wood (1993) attempted to examine the effects of and possible interactions between a user's cognitive and learning styles on the learning outcomes in a hypertext-based system. In their study, two standardized tests were used for identifying participants' cognitive style "field-dependence/independence" and learning style "serialist/holist." Holists are characterized as persons who prefer gaining an overview first while serialists are those who prefer establishing details before the overall picture. The participants were, first, asked to use a hypertext-based learning system to learn about given topics. After a learning period, participants' knowledge of the topics was evaluated. The results showed that serialists attempted to answer a higher number of questions and scored a higher number of correct answers in recall tests than holists did. Holists tended to answer fewer questions but more accurately than serialists. Field-independent participants tried a larger number of access attempts to information nodes than the field-dependents did. And the field-dependents were less successful in producing correct answers. Despite these differences, any effect on learning and recall was minimal. During an initial phase of adjustment to an information system, cognitive and learning styles affected ways of searching for information but eventually all participants managed to find ways to adapt to the new situation and achieved similar end results.

Holistic User-Oriented Studies

Studies with a more holistic approach are concerned with user's internal variables (cognitive, affective, or physical aspects) as well as external variables (social or cultural aspects). Since many user behaviors could not be clearly explained by cognitive aspects alone, researchers started to explore other possibilities.

Nahl and Tenopir (1996) provide a naturalistic study that examined novice's searching behavior in a full-text database. Seven novice searchers were asked to search information on any topic of interest and to "think aloud" while searching for the topic in a full-text database. Verbal protocols (as these "think aloud" sessions are called) and transaction logs that capture actual users' keystrokes and system responses were all used to record and analyze the novices' search behavior. Based on the recorded data, novice users' information needs and reactions to the information system were categorized into three groups: (1) cognitive, (2) affective, and (3) sensorimotor. Nearly half (48%) of the questions asked by novices were affectively-oriented ones while cognitively-oriented and sensorimotor-oriented questions accounted for about 26% each. These findings imply that the affective domain plays an important role in initiating information search.

Kuhlthau's (1991) six stages in the information seeking process (initiation, selection, exploration, formulation, collection, and presentation) has been used to shed further light on the affective dimension. She found that an information seeker's affective behavior changes depending on which stage the user has achieved. The studies of the user's cognitive behavior far outweigh those on the user's affective behavior, so there is much yet to be done to fully understand the changes in affective behavior.

Perhaps the best known work in determining the user's holistic dimension in information seeking is Dervin's "sense-making" approach which has developed from her perspective from the field of communication. According to Dervin, an information need is perceived when an individual's internal sense is "run out" (Dervin & Nilan, 1986). Using a three-part model that posits a "Situation," a "Gap," and finally a "Use or Help phase," she attempts to show how information needs vary over space and time. When individuals encounter a situation raising questions about their existing knowledge, they try to fill in the perceived gap or uncertainty by using sense-making. The sense-making effort is a process of using whatever is available to bridge the gap faced by the user, and the result of the process can vary depending on individuals. Jacobson's study (1991) of NEXIS users is a study on the use of information systems which applies Dervin's sense-making approach. In his research, participants who were novice users of information systems were asked to search for information on a given topic using NEXIS, a full-text information system. After the search session, participants had a time-line interview during which they were asked to describe their experience with the information system. The time-line interview is a method that Dervin developed to see when users perceive gaps and how they bridge the gaps. More detailed information on the method will be discussed later, in the methodology section of this paper. Jacobson found that there were four main stages of a search session: (1) choosing a library (a library in NEXIS denotes a family of files), (2) choosing a file or group within a library, (3) designing a search string and running the search, and (4) displaying the results. A much larger number of events were involved in each stage, and more than half (54%) of the events were perceived by the users to be successful. Information seeking behavior was distributed throughout the time-line of events. About 59% of the information seeking behaviors (or questioning) were observed when participants were successfully processing information with no difficulties in understanding the system. This suggests that questions asked by users while they use a system are not necessarily related to the problems of the system interface. Among questions concerned with the system interface, navigation was to be the most common problem for novice users of the system. Although, the study was not intended to evaluate a system, it provided useful information on the design of an information system as well as user's information seeking behavior.

Uses and gratifications theory, another theory from the field of communication, is worth considering in trying to understand the selection and use of information systems, the next step after identifying an information need. Research on uses and gratifications in mass communication media has focused on trying to explain how and why an audience selects a particular medium.

Cantril (1950) found that books are used for strengthening one's knowledge or understanding of self whereas films and TVs are used primarily for entertainment. This finding was confirmed by Katz et al. (1974). Their study found that printed materials were used for self-learning while television programming was preferred for entertainment. Lometi (1977) attempted to group different communication channels by type, and identified three clusters of channels used for different purposes: (1) printed materials were used for information gratification, (2) electronic channels for entertainment, and (3) interpersonal channels for behavioral and affective guidance.

In investigating reasons why a certain medium is preferred to others for a certain purpose, several models, mostly concerned with the affective domain of users (expectation, for example), have been developed. However, the current tendency is to explain media use behavior in the larger context, embracing psychological, social and cultural aspects. In the field of LIS, Chatman (1991) used uses and gratification theory to conduct a study observing how individuals in lower working class situations seek information. One of Chatman's findings was that the janitorial workers used media that could respond to their immediate and practical concerns. Television and newspapers were the preferred media since they provided information on ways to cope with insecurity that the workers experienced and relayed general information about everyday events.

Research on users of information systems, and perhaps even more appropriately the World Wide Web environment which seems to combine the features of an information system with many potentially entertaining visuals has yet to be studied using this gratification theory, but it seems plausible that the uses and gratification theory can enhance our understanding of individual's selection of as well as use behavior when there are a variety of different information channels from which to choose.

As the view of the user's position as a unit of analysis moves from a more marginal system component position to a much more centralized component of our field, the amount and type of user behavior research will increase dramatically. The foregoing review has been an effort to show just such a shift. From the early Cranfield studies where relevance was assumed to be static for all users to the most recent efforts concerned with users' dynamically changing affective responses to information systems, the methods needed have become more numerous and much more complex.

In what follows, we have attempted to highlight some of the methods frequently used for research in the area of users' information seeking behavior. It cannot be considered an exhaustive collection of methods, but is described here to suggest possible approaches to those who wish to undertake user studies.

SOME METHODOLOGIES FOR STUDYING USERS

There are dozens of methods available to examine the behavior of human subjects. In the LIS field, a large number of research studies depend upon the questionnaire or interview to determine what people think. We have tried in what follows to concentrate on other alternative approaches. Beginning with the experimental approach where much of a situation is carefully controlled and proceeding through several more subjective or qualitative methods where much of a situation is studied in its own natural setting, the researcher must realize that a method is often chosen because it offers the best approach for answering the research question posed. In making a decision about a research method, the research problem should always come first. Sometimes, it is useful to anticipate difficulties with a research effort by planning on the use of more than one method, so consider the following list of methods as something of a selection list.

Experiments

The experimental approach is one of the most powerful models for scientific inquiry. Laboratory experiments are often the model for experimental research efforts and they assume the possibility of a specially created setting in which the experimenter is able to control a wide variety of extraneous factors. Such settings are usually quite unlike a traditional information provision environment and if we choose to use these more realistic settings some of the control may be lost. A great deal of careful planning and literature review precedes the experimental plan. The variables to be measured and how they will be measured are both conceived in advance by the experimenter(s). The procedure of an experiment is well structured and controlled in order to prevent other intervening variables from biasing the results. The power of the experimental approach comes from the maximization of control and the randomization of participants, so that explanation of the results is more reliable and generalizable.

There are some drawbacks, however, for the experimental method. The experimental situation can be artificial and different from that experienced in a more realistic setting. This may mean that the findings from an experiment might not fully explain the events of a real situation. Unless all pertinent variables are identified before and observed in the experiment, one may not detect the more complex interactions occurring among different variables. Analysis of the data is usually done quantitatively. This quantitative assessment may uncover an observable tendency in the data and the likelihood that this tendency was not caused by chance alone, but only through many replications can some real understanding of the underlying phenomenon occur and a satisfying explanation of a complex relationship be found.

A recent example of an experimental effort to examine the user's cognitive behavior in information seeking is found in Allen (1992). In his study, he used college undergraduates and randomly assigned them to experimental treatments that tested the effects of their cognitive abilities like vocabulary comprehension, logical reasoning, and spatial orientation on their ability to use a bibliographic retrieval system. Particularly, he found that vocabulary comprehension has an effect on the willingness of people to express their information needs in alternative ways.

Good experimental research is difficult in the LIS field because the need to create a single experimental effect often means that subjects recruited must be placed in information use settings where artificial information needs are imposed upon them. To use an information seeker's own information need seems to require more subjective techniques which enable more of a focus on the individual's unique state of being.

Interview Techniques

Focus Groups

Focus groups represent an informal approach to providing a planned discussion designed to determining the needs and feelings of a particular population. Members of the focus group are chosen because they are assumed to represent well the population to be addressed. Focus groups are often used as a preliminary step in the development of questionnaires or interviews in order to determine whether definitions, terms, concepts to be used will be appropriate to the sample who will later receive the questionnaire. Sometimes, however, the focus group can be a study in itself, rather than a precursor to other data collection efforts. A focus group usually consists of six to nine individuals and they discuss their experience, suggestions, and other issues related fairly specifically to discussion questions designed by the researchers in advance. A moderator initiates the discussion along these pre-planned guidelines, but needs to provide fairly unobtrusive guidance. For example, the moderator has to identify what issues are to be discussed and set goals for the kinds of information to be gathered, but the flow of the discussion should occur without too many interruptions from the moderator. Focus groups are usually audio taped with the participants' permission and reviewed later for the extraction of themes and content areas that may have emerged during the discussion and that may not have been in the moderator's original plan (Krueger, 1988).

Naturalistic Inquiry

Mellon (1990) was a strong voice in LIS research advocating a group of techniques that first arose in other social science disciplines like sociology and anthropology. These techniques have been variously described as naturalistic, ethnographic, qualitative, symbolic interactionism–and to the various disciplines from which these traditions arose, there are fine distinctions between these differing names. But common to all is the general central ideal of collecting naturally occurring data–that is, data that arise from a natural context and environment. In user studies, this has come to mean going to environments where users experience need for information rather than studying the behavior of users only within an existing information system environment. These more subjective, qualitative methods seek to find broader explanations than can be achieved by looking at the relationship between two highly controlled variables in an experimental setting. The differences between the qualitative and the quantitative approaches are well documented and two well respected guides can be found in Silverman's (1993) and Erlandson et al.'s (1993) works.

Essentially the differences in approach between the quantitative and qualitative camps makes them good partners. Qualitative approaches use narrative description and seek to find categories that emerge as the research proceeds. Quantitative or experimental approaches require that concretely operationalized variables be determined before the study begins and may depend upon some sort of intervention that creates a very unrealistic environment for the respondent so that other variables are kept from interfering. Some compelling naturalistic studies of users' information seeking characteristics have been done by Chatman (1991), Kwasnik (1991) and Erdelez (1995). In these examples, respondents' opinions about information seeking and information organization were gathered through long in-depth interviews. The participants in each of these studies were purposefully selected to reflect a particular group of information users. Such purposive samples are the rule in naturalistic inquiry as opposed to the more randomly assigned participants used in experimental research studies.

Time-Line Interviews (for Dervin's Sense-Making Approach)

Somewhat similar to the naturalistic approach above, the influence of Brenda Dervin's (1992) sense-making has been substantial upon the information user research in the LIS field. Her work, and the many studies which use her sense-making techniques, have argued from the early 1970s that users should not be considered in aggregate groups–that each user constructs sense or meaning from a particularly personal point of view and from a particular moment in time.

According to Dervin, information-seeking can be defined as "gap bridging." The "time-line" interview method has been developed for gathering information on the gaps and gap-bridging that the user perceives. The "time-line" interview refers to a structured interview during which users are asked to describe what they have experienced in a small segment of time. At times, the respondent is asked to imagine that they are making a movie of the event–and to imagine what was occurring in scene 1, etc. The "movie" might be conceived as an information search effort. In the time-line interview, individuals are asked to recount what they experienced as if it were "a series of snapshots conveying everything that happened." Then, the interviewer writes down each event on a card. Once all the events are identified and written down, the interviewer goes through the whole series of events one at a time, and asks the respondent more detailed questions about their experiences at each snapshot point.

An effective demonstration of this approach is given in Newby, Nilan and Duvall (1991). They show how this more situational approach can be effective at explaining user behavior as they learn a word processing product. The authors argue that the user-based situational time line does a better job of predicting the information needed for a specific task and also provides system designers with detailed data about the nature of the task process in a dynamic, user-centered form along with a time-based specification of the information needs associated with each step in the task process.

Written User Surveys

According to a recently published content analysis of current LIS research on information use and users by Julien (1996), 44% of the research in this area is still conducted using the survey method. It has been one of the most frequently used methodologies for our field, perhaps because of its convenience and ability to be conducted without undue intervention in the lives of respondents. Information on users can be acquired simply by asking questions of users, but obtaining meaningful data requires careful thought about questionnaire content. Questionnaires can be distributed directly to individuals to be answered as they leave or while they visit an information setting; this approach results in a convenience sample and there are often difficulties generalizing to a broader population from such samples. For this reason, questionnaires are often administered by mail, to a selected sample which is drawn to be more representative of some larger population. The disadvantage is that the recipient may not complete and return the survey, but generally the benefits of allowing the respondent to choose the time when they can best give the questionnaire their attention and provide thoughtful responses outweigh the lack of response disadvantages.

With the advent of Internet technologies, questionnaires can also be e-mailed, or made available through the use of a Web page. Some early examples of efforts to place questionnaires on the Web are Palmquist (1996) and Bertot and McClure (1996). In both studies, low response rates affected the success of the Web approach. In the case of questionnaires offered through a Web page, a variety of issues arise—the adequacy of recipients' computer technology for responding in a technically reliable manner, the accurate identity of the recipient/respondent, the accuracy of the data they supply, the generalizability of results, etc. But the one clear advantage that the Web approach permits is that the same software that formats the questionnaire can also create a database of the responses. This allows an automatically created record of the survey responses that can be passed on to a statistical package, potentially saving hours of laborious coding of the responses.

Transaction Log Analysis

Transaction logging involves the automatic collection of computer use statistics concerning the human-computer interactions that have occurred while the system was being used (Nielsen, 1993). Log analysis is often used for collecting information about the actual use of a system. The advantage of this method is that it can record every keystroke and machine response that system users experience and do so unobtrusively. The disadvantage is that since all transactions are automatically logged it can be difficult to determine when one user completes an interaction and another user begins. Also, without some effort to accompany the transaction log with a user's verbal "talk aloud" data, the transaction log cannot provide any cognitive or emotional data on the user's internal state. At best, transaction logs tell us more about systems and should be viewed as a supplement to user study methods rather than a central approach. Additional information through some form of personal monitoring or taping of a user's internal state or intention is needed before systems can be more respondent to users.

Unconscious Cognition

A recent dissertation (Ballesteros, 1995) at the University of Texas at Austin has introduced to the LIS literature a new approach to the elicitation of users' needs. Much of the research in users' needs assumes the importance of conscious cognition by the user, but Ballesteros felt that the present theory of conscious information needs did not explain sufficiently the problems demonstrated by users, particularly at the outset of an inquiry, of articulating an information need. In her research, unconscious cognition was tapped with a programmed relaxation device that took the user through a 20-minute, deep relaxation experience that elicited an altered state of consciousness which she monitored with an electroencephalographic biofeedback program. Prior to the relaxation exercise, the participants were asked to describe a present problem on which they were working. The subjects receiving the experimental treatment reported increases in intuition, insight, ideas and a more holistic understanding of their respective problems. While we may be some years away from such equipment at the reference desk, the effect and impact of the method on needs elicitation seems well worth additional research effort.

Usability

The term usability comes from the systems testing work conducted by many commercial software developers. Long aware of the problems that users report concerning software that is less than friendly or that fails to support the users' cognitive view of the task to be completed, software engineers sought to develop techniques for evaluating the usability of a product. Often applied primarily to interface design and development activities, usability studies involve a wide variety of techniques. Of particular merit for the task capturing users' models of software capabilities, a technique called "the cognitive walkthrough" has evolved as an important usability testing mechanism. Generally concerned with novice users, the cognitive walkthrough focuses on only one attribute of usability, the ease of learning a system. Theories of skill acquisition (Anderson, 1987) predict that facilitating learning by exploration will facilitate skill acquisition. Cognitive walkthroughs evaluate each step necessary to perform a task. They attempt to uncover design flaws that would interfere with learning by having the user carry out a task description and assess the sequence of actions that the user goes through to attempt a successful performance of the designated task. Each step in a performance sequence is examined to see if the user associates the correct action with the effect that the user was trying to achieve. Nielsen and Mack (1994) provide a comprehensive guide to a wide variety of usability methods and to a host of published research examples which demonstrated the effectiveness of such methods.

Verbal Protocol Analysis

In the 1980s, the evolution of the interdisciplinary studies called "cognitive science" meant an increased interest in studying the cognitive activity of many groups–in education, in human/computer studies, in psychology, etc. Concurrent and retrospective verbal reports were seen as methods of determining subjects' cognitive processes while they pursued particular tasks. Often conducted in more laboratory-like settings, these verbal reports have now become a standard research method in many disciplines. Concurrent verbalization was the phrase given to the technique of evoking a temporal sequence of mental events, also called "talk aloud" protocols. The standard approach to getting the subject to verbalize their thoughts concurrently is to instruct them to "think aloud." Retrospective verbalizations have a role to play in the development of oral histories within the LIS literature. Ericsson and Simon (1993) provide an excellent guide to evoking and analyzing verbal protocol data although they do advise the researcher about to examine the wealth of guidance available that there are a wide variety of instructions and procedures used to elicit concurrent and retrospective verbalizations. Their own techniques should not be taken as definitive.

Raya Fidel (1988) used verbal protocols and transaction logs of searches in order to examine professional searchers who were using bibliographic databases as a regular part of their work day. The purpose of her study was to identify, through these verbal "think aloud" protocols, whether searchers developed intuitive rules to guide their decisions about the selection of search terms.

CONCLUSION

As a discipline, library and information science must improve its understanding of the cognitive and contextual needs of information seekers. The intra-personal psychological understandings that move users to address information needs with the use of an information system are still not well understood. Inspired by the interdisciplinarity of LIS research methods, a variety of approaches have evolved which allow particular insights into the users' information-seeking strategies. The movement of the information services toward a less paper-based environment seems to dictate an increasing likelihood that the role of information counselor and trainer will increase for LIS professionals. These roles have previously been less than central to professional tasks since the central issues were based upon the organization and maintenance of the collection. While a more user-oriented research perspective is not new to our field, there have been few identifiable techniques that were available to the working LIS profession and that could be applied toward understanding a particular user community. User data collection has traditionally centered around those elements of the collection and its organization so that data could be easily collected, and most importantly collected with the least intrusion upon the user. The materials collection, as a defining feature of information service, gave rise to techniques that checked the correctness of users interactions. The profession now needs to shift its emphasis to understanding why the user behaves as he or she does. The data gathered through more traditional collection use studies did more to explain collection-centered questions but did little to identify more individually held user concerns.

We have attempted to review studies on use and users of information systems and to describe research techniques currently in use within the LIS research community. We could not be exhaustive in our coverage and sought to focus on those techniques that seem to hold promise for identifying users internal states of being as they seek information. Future user studies should try to go beyond simply describing users' collection choices, and to aim at understanding and predicting users and their interactions with information retrieval systems. For this sort of understanding, those practicing in the information services should be able to choose from a variety of methods to test existing theories in order to increase our common pool of information of user-centered data with which to build a better understanding of our role and our user communities.

REFERENCES

Allen, Bryce. (1992) "Cognitive differences in end-user searching of a CD-ROM index." In: *15th International Conference on Research and Development in Information Retrieval.* Baltimore: Association of Computing Machinery.

Anderson, J.R. (1987) "Skill acquisition: Compilation of weak-method solutions." *Psychological Review* Vol. 94: p. 192-211.

Ballesteros, E.R. (1995) "Unconscious Cognition in the Conduct of Inquiry: An Information Counseling Approach," Ph.D. Thesis. The University of Texas.

Belkin, N.J. (1980) "Anomalous state of knowledge as a basis for information retrieval." *Canadian Journal of Information Science* Vol. 5: p. 133-144.

Belkin, N.J. & Robertson, S. (1976) "Information science and the phenomenon of information," *Journal of the American Society for Information Science (JASIS)* 27: p. 197-210.

Bertot, J.C. & McClure, C.R. (1996) "Electronic Surveys: Methodological Implications for Using the World Wide Web to Collect Survey Data." In: Hardin, S. (ed.) *Global Complexity: Information, Chaos and Control: Proceedings of the 59th Annual Meeting of the American Society for Information Science,* Vol. 33: p. 173-185.

Borgman, C. (1984) "Psychological research in human-computer interaction," *Annual Review of Information Science and Technology (ARIST)* Vol. 19: p. 30-64.

Brown, M.E. (1991) "A general model of information-seeking behavior," *Proceedings of the 54th ASIS Annual Meeting* p. 9-14.

Cantril, H. (1950) *The "Why" of Man's Experience*. New York: Macmillan.

Campagnoni, F.R. & Ehrlich, K. (1989) "Information retrieval using hypertext-based help system," *Proceedings of the 12th Annual International ACMSIGIR Conference* p. 212-220.

Carbonell, N.J. (1986) "User modelling techniques," *International Journal of Man-Machine Studies* Vol. 24: p. 29-38.

Chatman, E.A. (1991) "Life in a small world: Applicability of gratification theory to information-seeking behavior," *JASIS* 46(6): p. 438-449.

Daniels, P.J. (1986) "Cognitive models in information retrieval an evaluative review," *Journal of Documentation* 42(4): p. 272-304.

Dervin, B. (1992) "From the Mind's Eye of the User: The Sense-Making Qualitative-Quantitative Methodology." In: Glazier, J.D. & Powell, R. (eds.) *Qualitative research in information management*. Englewood, CO: Libraries Unlimited, p. 61-84.

Dervin, B. & Nilan, M. (1986) "Information needs and users," *ARIST* Vol. 21: p. 3-33.

Ellis, D., Ford, N. & Wood, F. (1993) "Hypertext and learning styles," *The Electronic Library* 11(1): p. 13-18.

Erdelez, S. (1995) "Information Encountering: An Explanation Beyond Information Seeking," Ph.D. Thesis. Syracuse University.

Ericsson, K.A. and H.A. Simon. (1993) *Protocol analysis: Verbal reports as data*. Cambridge, MA: MIT Press.

Erlandson, D.A., Harris, E.L., Skipper, B.L. & Allen, S.D. (1993) *Doing naturalistic inquiry: A guide to methods*. Newbury Park, CA: Sage.

Fidel, R. (1988) "Factors affecting the selection of search keys." In *Information Technology: Planning for the Second Fifty Years, Proceedings of the 51st Annual Meeting of the American Society for Information Science*. Medford, NJ: Learned Information, 76-79.

Goldstein, K.M. & Blackman, S. (1978) *Cognitive style: Five approaches and relevant research*. New York: John Wiley.

Jacobson, T.L. (1991) "Sense-making in a database environment," *Information Processing & Management* 27(6): p. 647-657.

Johnson-Laird, P. (1983) *Mental models: Towards a cognitive science of language, interface and consciousness*. Cambridge: Cambridge University Press.

Julien, H. (1996) "A Content analysis of the recent information needs and uses literature," *Library and Information Science Research* 18: p. 53-65.

Katz, E.B., Blumler, J.G., & Gurevitch, M. (1974) "Utilization of mass communication by the individual," In: Blumler, J.G. & Katz, E. (eds.) *The use of mass communication*. Beverly Hills, CA: Sage. p. 19-32.

Korthauer, R.D. & Koubek, R.J. (1994) "An empirical evaluation of knowledge, cognitive style, and structure upon the performance of hypertext task," *International Journal of Human-Computer Interaction* 6(4): p. 373-390.

Krikelas, J. (1983) "Information-seeking behavior: Patterns and concepts," *Drexel Library Quarterly* Vol. 19: p. 5-22.

Krueger, R.A. (1988) *Focus groups: A practical guide for applied research* Newbury Park, CA: Sage.

Kuhlthau, C.C. (1991) "Inside the search process: information seeking from the user's perspective," *JASIS* 42(5): p. 361-371.

Kwasnik, B.H. (1991) "The importance of factors that are not document attributes in the organization of personal documents," *Journal of Documentation* 47(4): p. 389-398.

Lometi, G.E. et al. (1977) "Investigating the assumptions of uses and gratifications research," *Communication Research* Vol. 4: p. 321-338.

Marchionini, G., Lin. X. & Dwiggins, S. (1990) "Effects of search and subject expertise on information seeking in a hypertext environment," *Proceedings of the 53rd Annual Meeting of the ASIS* p. 129-142.

Markey, K. (1984) *Subject searching in library catalogs: Before and after the introduction of online catalog.* Dublin, OH: OCLC.

Martens, K. (1979) "Cognitive style: An introduction with annotated bibliography," paper presented at the American College Personnel Association Convention, Atlanta, GA.

Matthews, J.R., Lawrence, G.S. & Freguson, D.K. (1983) *Using online catalogs: A nationwide survey.* New York: Neal-Schumann.

Mellon, C. (1990) *Naturalistic inquiry for Library Science: Methods and application for research, evaluation, and teaching.* New York: Greenwood Press.

Messick, S. (1976) "Personality consistencies in cognition and creativity," In: Messick, S. (ed.) *Individuality in learning: Implications of cognitive style and creativity for human development* San Francisco: Jossey-Bass.

Messick, (1970) "The criterion problem in the evaluation of instruction: Assessing possible, not just intended, outcomes," In: Wittrock, M.C. & Wiley, D. *The evaluation of instruction: Issues and problems.* New York: Holt, Reinhart, and Winston.

Nahl, D. & Tenopir, C. (1996) "Affective and cognitive searching behavior of novice end-users of a full-text database," *JASIS* 47(4): p. 276-286.

Newby, B., Nilan, M. and Duvall, L. (1991) "Toward a reassessment of individual differences for information systems: The power of user-based situational predictors." In: *Proceedings of the 54th Annual Meeting of the American Society for Information Science.* Washington, DC, 73-81.

Nielsen, J. (1993) *Usability engineering.* New York: Academic Press.

Nielsen, J. & Mack, R.L. (1994) *Usability Inspection Methods.* New York: John Wiley and Sons.

Palmquist, R.A. (1996) "The Search for an Internet Metaphor: A Comparison of Literatures." In: Hardin, S. (ed.) *Global Complexity: Information, Chaos and Control. Proceedings of the 59th Annual Meeting of the American Society for Information Science,* Vol. 33: p. 198-202.

Rich, E. (1983) "Users and individuals: individualizing user models," *International Journal of Man-Machine Studies* Vol. 18: p. 199-214.

Rouse, W.B. & Rouse, S.H. (1984) "Human information seeking and design of information systems," *Information Processing & Management* 20(1-2): p. 129-138.

Silverman, David. (1993) *Interpreting Qualitative Data: Methods for analysing talk, text and interaction.* London: Sage.

Sleeman, D. (1985) "UMFE: A user modeling front-end subsystem," *International Journal of Man-Machine Studies* Vol. 23: p. 71-88.

Sparck Jones, K. (1986) "Issues in user modeling for expert systems," In: Cohn, A.G. & Thomas, J.R. (eds.) *Artificial intelligence and its applications.* p. 183-195.

Sugar, W. (1995) "User-centered perspective of information retrieval research and analysis methods," *ARIST* Vol. 30: p. 77-109.

Taylor, R.S. (1968) "Question negotiation and information seeking in libraries," *College and Research Libraries* 178-194.

Witkin, H.A. (1978) *Cognitive styles in personal and cultural adaptation.* Washington, D.C.: Clark University Press.

INTERNET:
ORGANIZATION AND SEARCHING

The Retrieval Power
of Selected Search Engines:
How Well Do They Address
General Reference Questions
and Subject Questions?

Ingrid Hsieh-Yee

SUMMARY. This study evaluates how well eight major search engines produced answers to twenty-one real reference questions and

Ingrid Hsieh-Yee is Associate Professor, School of Library and Information Studies, Catholic University of America, Washington, D.C. 20064. E-mail: hsiehyee@cua.edu

Harriet Nelson, the Head of Reference Services of the John K. Mullen of Denver Memorial Library, and her staff collected the reference questions. Three students, Teria Curry, Grace Garbe, and John Barry Trott, conducted most of the searches for this study. Their generous assistance is gratefully acknowledged.

[Haworth co-indexing entry note]: "The Retrieval Power of Selected Search Engines: How Well Do They Address General Reference Questions and Subject Questions?" Hsieh-Yee, Ingrid. Co-published simultaneously in *The Reference Librarian* (The Haworth Press, Inc.) No. 60, 1998, pp. 27-47; and: *Electronic Resources: Use and User Behavior* (ed: Hemalata Iyer) The Haworth Press, Inc., 1998, pp. 27-47. Single or multiple copies of this article are available for a fee from The Haworth Document Delivery Service [1-800-342-9678, 9:00 a.m. - 5:00 p.m. (EST). E-mail address: getinfo@haworth.com].

five made-up subject questions. The retrieval and relevancy-ranking abilities of search engines were measured by precision, duplicate, most-relevant-item score, and relevancy-ranking score. Search engines did not produce good results for the reference questions, but did well with the subject questions. T-tests found the two types of questions quite different in nature, so the best engines were identified by the type of questions. Open Text was the best in handling the reference questions, and InfoSeek was the best at answering subject questions. *[Article copies available for a fee from The Haworth Document Delivery Service: 1-800-342-9678. E-mail address: getinfo@haworth.com]*

INTRODUCTION

The growth of the Internet has been dramatic. According to the July 1996 "Domain Survey," the exponential growth is continuing: the Net is estimated to double in size about every 12 to 15 months (Lottor, 1996). Internet Solutions also reported dramatic growth of the World Wide Web. In their estimate, there were 100,000 Web sites (domain) in August of 1995, and the number went up to 536,041 by August 1996 (1996). Since each site can host many Web pages, this translates into many times more Web pages. Granted, the quality of many pages can be questioned and the maintenance of many pages is sporadic, but there are credible pages that offer valuable information on many subjects. What users need is a filtering system to separate the wheat from the chaff.

Various attempts have been made to facilitate this task. Librarians and subject specialists have compiled subject guides. *College & Research Libraries News* periodically publishes Internet resource guides on selected topics; and the Clearinghouse of Subject-Oriented Internet Resources now covers more than 400 subjects (Argus, 1996). In addition, catalogers have created InterCat, an experimental catalog for the Internet (OCLC, 1995). OCLC has also produced a database, NetFirst, to index Internet resources with Library of Congress subject headings and Dewey Decimal Classification numbers (OCLC, 1996). Reference librarians have started InfoFilter, a Web site, to share reviews of Internet resources; and librarians have experimented with subject classification to organize Internet resources (see, for example, BUBL's Subject Tree and McKiernan's CyberStacks). But the effort that has received most attention from Internet users is probably the spiders and robots that are driving the search services. For many Internet searchers these engines offer a temporary relief, giving them a way into the huge information space. They soon realize, however, that these engines are not perfect because they cover different territories (with some areas of overlap, of course), index differently, and retrieve items by keywords. Users can never have the confidence that a search is comprehensive or conclusive. Although the huge retrieval results are supposedly ranked by relevance, users continue to struggle with false drops, duplicates, and irrelevant items. On the whole, good progress has been made in helping users to navigate the Internet; but the tools are so numerous that choosing the right one becomes a task.

Furthermore, the selection of proper search engines may become more important, for general users and librarians alike, because of a troubling trend. InfoSeek, for instance, has a free service, but its fee-based service, InfoSeek Professional, offers a bigger index and more powerful search features; WebCrawler was acquired by America Online and a subscription requirement could be imposed someday. If this movement toward fee for service becomes a trend, it will be necessary for users, and librarians in particular, to know which engines to use.

It is in this context that the present study was designed. This study attempted to assess the effectiveness of search engines in addressing information needs. Can they retrieve answers to real reference questions? Do they produce good results for subject questions? How well does their ranking of retrieved items approximate users' relevance assessment? Which search engines perform best? Answers to these questions will help us understand the strengths and limitations of search engines better and enable us to select appropriate search engines to meet our information needs.

LITERATURE REVIEW

Many search engines are available and can be easily accessed. Netscape's "Net Search" and Library of Congress's "WWW by Subject or Keyword" both bring together major search engines. There are also meta-engines that allow searchers to access several search engines quickly, but only "Savvy Search" is able to search up to five databases at a time. "All-in-One" represents another group of tools that present the search forms of many search engines on one Web site to make searching easier.

The operation of spiders, robots, and other automated programs was summarized by Prosise (1996), and the limitations of these tools were analyzed by Koster (1995). Several papers purported to evaluate Internet search tools, but most of them offered descriptions of the World Wide Web or search engines. Brinkley and Burke (1995) described Hytelnet, Archie, Gopher, WAIS and the World Wide Web. Courtois, Baer, and Stark (1995) used three queries to test the search engines and Web indexes, but their report is mostly descriptive in nature. Kimmel (1996) presented valuable profiles of robot-generated databases and offered novice searchers a good guide to search engines. Venditto (1996) tested seven search engines and described their search features. Similar reports abound on the Internet and many of them can be found on Campbell's list (1996). A few good examples are the reports of Lin (1995), Winship (1995), and Webster and Paul (1995).

There have been relatively few evaluation studies that involved field-testing search engines. Desai tested the retrieval power of thirteen search tools with one query (1995). By searching his name, he was able to determine how many of his Web documents were retrieved. InfoSeek and Lycos performed best by retrieving seven of the twenty-four documents, while other engines and indexes such as WebCrawler, World Wide Web Worm and Yahoo! fared poorly. Leighton compared the performance of InfoSeek, Lycos, WebCrawler, and World Wide Web Worm using eight questions (1995). He experimented with four measures–duplicate ratio, precision, total precision, and top ten precision–and concluded that Lycos and InfoSeek performed better than the others. Packer and Tomaiuolo (1996) searched 200 reference questions in Alta Vista, Magellan, Info-Seek, Lycos and Point. Their precision score was based on the first ten items retrieved, and they found Alta Vista to be the best performer, followed by InfoSeek, Lycos, Magellan, and Point. Meghabghab and Meghabghab (1996) used five queries to test five search engines, performing basic and refined searches in each engine. They modified Leighton's top ten precision by using the top twenty-five as the base and added the number of "promising pages" to the precision score to create another measure. They found Yahoo! to be the best performer. Findings of these studies do not conclusively pinpoint the best search engine because different questions, different number of questions, and different measures were used for evaluation. Nevertheless, these studies demonstrated various ways of evaluating search engines and offered reasonable new measures of search performance.

RESEARCH QUESTIONS

The present study differed from previous studies in that it focused on two types of questions: reference questions collected at a reference desk and subject questions made up for this study. It also modified two previous measures and introduced two new measures to assess search engines' relevancy ranking. The design of the study was guided by these research questions:

- How well can search engines produce answers for general reference questions? Which search engines are the top three in answering this type of question?
- How well can search engines retrieve information for subject questions? Which search engines are the top three in answering this type of question?
- Do search engines perform differently for general reference questions and subject questions?
- Do search engines perform differently for real subject reference questions and made-up subject questions?

METHODOLOGY

The study evaluated eight search engines that are well known and free to the public. They included Alta Vista, Excite, InfoSeek Guide, Lycos, Magellan, Open Text, WebCrawler, and World Wide Web Worm. Many factors can contribute to the success of a search: a good understanding of the search request, searcher's strategy, database, search engine, and relevance judgment by the searcher. In this study several of these factors were controlled so that the search engine differences could be observed.

Search engines vary by the size and contents of their databases, their indexing policies, quality control, retrieval methods and presentation of search results. It is understood that test questions with different complexity and specificity will be more likely to be valid in identifying the best search engine. Nevertheless, previous studies suggest that there may not be a search engine that is better than others in answering all types of questions. We standardized the search requests by using twenty questions collected at the reference desk of the John K. Mullen of Denver Library of the Catholic University of America and five subject questions that were developed in areas that have had many Internet resources–entertainment, business, politics, finance, and health. The collected reference questions included specific queries and broad topical queries and were believed to be valid in testing search engines' ability to answer real reference questions. The five subject questions were artificial, but this design enabled us to perform more meaningful analyses. After all, no evaluation would be very insightful if we used questions for which nothing could be retrieved.

Data collection. The eight search engines were assigned to four searchers to ensure that each question was searched twice in each engine. Searchers were instructed to use Netscape to access the World Wide Web, to search given questions in the designated search engines, and to produce printouts for search results. Searches began in April and concluded in June of 1996. The reference questions were slightly re-worded for Internet searches (see Appendix A). To make sure similar strategies were used, key terms were identified and basic parameters were given on how each search engine should be searched (see Appendix B). Searchers were also told to use their best judgment in assessing the relevance of retrieved items.

One reference question has two parts, so a total of twenty-one reference questions were used. Each of the twenty-one reference questions and five subject questions was searched twice in each search engine, but four times in Excite because it allows searches to be done by keyword and by concept. Midway through the data collection period Magellan began offering searchers the option of searching the rated portion of their database or the entire database. For the sake of consistency all searchers of Magellan were done in the entire database. A total of 468 searches were conducted.

Dependent variables. Four variables were measured for the study. "Precision" is traditionally defined as the number of relevant items retrieved divided by the number of items retrieved and has been a standard measure of information retrieval systems (Boyce, Meadow, and Kraft, 1994). Since it would be infeasible to evaluate the relevancy of the large number of pages retrieved by search engines, the study operationalized this variable as

$$\text{Precision: } \frac{\text{the number of relevant items in the first 10 items}}{\text{the first 10 items}}$$

The first-ten-item approach can be justified because these items are most likely to be viewed by searchers. This measure was used by Leighton (1995) and Packer and Tomaiuolo (1996). But unlike Leighton's study, this study included duplicates and mirror sites in the precision measure because they were potentially useful (if what was duplicated was relevant) and eliminating them would make the base for comparison (which was ten) even smaller.

"Duplicate": In the early days of search engines there were anecdotal reports of duplicates, so this variable was included in our assessment. Duplicate was operationally defined as the number of items that repeat items that were presented before them. Mirror sites were counted as duplicates. In this study we used the number of duplicates based on the first ten items retrieved. It is slightly different from the duplicate ratio in Leighton's study.

"Most-relevant-item score" (MRI): All of the selected search engines rank retrieval results, using different algorithm, and present best matches first, but the ranking has not always been helpful. This variable was designed to examine the ranking ability of search engines. It is based on the assumption that an effective ranking procedure would place the most relevant item at the top of the retrieval result. Operationally, searchers identified the most relevant item from the first ten items and gave it a score for its location. If the item appeared as the first, second, or third item on the list, the engine would receive a score of 1, 2, or 3. If the item appeared elsewhere, a score of "6" was given. The value "6" was chosen because it indicated that the item was placed out of the first half of a ten-item retrieval. The lower the MRI score, the better an engine was in ranking a most relevant item.

"Relevancy-ranking score" (RR): This variable also evaluate relevancy ranking of search engines, but in a different way. It was defined as the percentage of relevant items that appeared in the first half of the ten-item list. It is based on the assumption that relevancy of items would decrease as one goes down a properly ranked list. Searchers recorded the number of relevant items in each half of the ten-item list, and the investigator converted the numbers according to the following formula to arrive at a relevancy-ranking score:

$$\frac{\text{the number of relevant items in the first half of the list}}{\text{the total number of relevant items in the ten-item list}} \times 100\%$$

"Recall" is another standard measure for information retrieval and is defined as the number of relevant items retrieved divided by the total number of relevant items in an information file (Boyce et al., 1994). This measure has been difficult to use because researchers need to identify all relevant items in an entire database or catalog. Such difficulty is compounded in the World Wide Web. With hundreds of thousands of Web pages indexed by the selected search engines it becomes infeasible to identify all Web pages relevant to a search topic. The possibility of a pooled base to calculate the revised recall score was considered and abandoned because of the large number of Web pages involved. Recall, therefore, was not used in this study.

Data analysis. From the 468 searches conducted, the four measures were recorded for each search under each engine. Frequency and average of these measures were calculated for each search engine by types of questions.

FINDINGS

Precision

The general reference questions were diverse, and a reference librarian would perhaps not use the Internet to find answers to some of them.

Nevertheless, all questions were searched in the search engines to assess their ability to answer real reference questions. Search engines did not do well. The average precision scores were very low, ranging from 0.31 to 2.93 (see Table 1). Open Text retrieved the highest number of relevant items, followed by Alta Vista and InfoSeek, with Lycos as a very close 4th. To show another dimension of the searches, data on each engine's zero hits were included in Table 1, indicting that Excite had the lowest number of zero hits, followed by Open Text and Lycos. Taken together, these two sets of data identified Open Text as the best engine in handling general reference questions; it usually retrieved Web pages for these questions and its search results had the highest precision score.

Search engines did better with the subject questions made up for this study. The lowest average precision score (3.2) was higher than the highest average precision score (2.93) for reference questions searches; and the highest precision score was 7.3 (see Table 2). InfoSeek performed best, followed by Magellan and Open Text, again with Lycos as a close fourth. Since these subject questions were designed for areas about which there is much information on the Internet, it was no surprise that the problem of zero hits was not as serious as that in the searches for reference questions (see Table 2). To take into account the quality of the items retrieved, "special precision," the frequency of searches that retrieved more than five relevant items were included in Table 2. InfoSeek again emerged as the winner, followed by Magellan, with Open Text, Lycos and WebCrawler tied for the third spot. These data show that InfoSeek was the best at

TABLE 1. Search engines' average precision and zero hits data for reference questions (N = 42, for Excite N_E = 44).

Engine	Precision (mean)	Zero Hits (frequency)	(percent)
Alta Vista	2.05	21	(50%)
Excite	1.75	12	(29%)
InfoSeek	1.95	19	(45%)
Lycos	1.93	16	(38%)
Magellan	1.33	27	(64%)
Open Text	2.93	15	(36%)
WebCrawler	1.10	24	(57%)
WWW Worm	0.31	32	(76%)

TABLE 2. Search engines' average precision, zero hits frequency, and special precision frequency for subject questions (N = 10, for Excite N_E = 12).

Engine	Precision (mean)	Zero hits (frequency)	Special precision[a] (frequency)
Alta Vista	5.4	0	3
Excite	4.2	1	3
InfoSeek	7.3	1	8
Lycos	6.3	0	6
Magellan	6.7	1	7
Open Text	6.5	2	6
WebCrawler	5.3	0	6
WWW Worm	3.2	5	2

[a]"Special precision" refers to the number of searches that retrieved more than 5 relevant items.

handing subject questions: it retrieved more than five relevant items for most of the subject questions and its search results had the highest precision score.

The precision data for reference questions and those for the subject questions presented different performance results. If the data were combined, Open Text (average precision 3.6) and InfoSeek (average precision 3.0) would be the top two search engines. But if the questions were distinctly different and search engines were responding to them differently, it might be more meaningful to evaluate the search engines by question types. To determine whether precision scores for both types of questions should be combined to measure the retrieval power of the search engines, t-tests were performed. The test significance was set at the level of .05. All of the test results rejected the null hypotheses of no difference, meaning that significant differences existed between these two types of questions (see Table 3 for a summary of the t-test results). It is therefore best that the search engines' precision power be represented according to types of questions. Figure 1 presents the precision scores of the search engines by question type.

The twenty-one general reference questions do include several topical questions and search engines' precision scores for them were compared with those for the five made-up subject questions to determine if search engines handle subject searches in a consistent manner. T-tests were performed and the test significance was set at the .05 level. Five of the eight

TABLE 3. T-tests that compared the average precision scores for reference questions and subject questions ($N_{ref} = 42$, $N_{sub} = 10$; for Excite $N_{refE} = 44$ and $N_{subE} = 12$).

Engine	T-test statistic	Probability
Alta Vista	3.218	0.002
Excite	2.954	0.005
InfoSeek	5.387	0.000
Lycos	4.466	0.000
Magellan	5.369	0.000
Open Text	2.992	0.004
WebCrawler	5.600	0.000
WWW Worm	4.831	0.000

$p < .05$

FIGURE 1

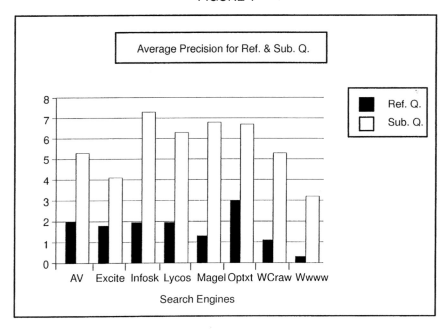

test results rejected the null hypotheses of no difference, meaning that five search engines (InfoSeek, Lycos, Magellan, WebCrawler, and World Wide Web Worm) searched these two groups of subject questions differently (see Table 4 for a summary of t-test results). To be conservative in our reporting, it was decided that precision scores for these two groups of subject questions would not be combined. This finding confirms a concern for this type of evaluation research: since search engines do not index the same information space and some topic areas have more Internet resources than others, the test questions used for evaluation may have much to do with evaluation results. Ideally researchers should identify the information space that is indexed by all search engines and develop questions from that space. This commonly indexed information space unfortunately is hard to pinpoint.

Duplicate

Duplicates in retrieval waste searchers' time and cause unnecessary confusion. In spite of anecdotal complaints about duplicates, however, the problem seemed to have been addressed by most search engines by 1996. For both the reference questions and the subject questions the average number of duplicates in each search engine was negligible (less than one). Since the subject questions had more hits, their chances for having duplicates were higher. The data show, however, that duplicates were not a

TABLE 4. T-tests that compared the average precision scores for real subject questions and made-up subject questions (N_{real} = 16, $N_{made-up}$ = 10; for Excite N_{realE} = 18, $N_{made-upE}$ = 12).

Engine	T-test statistic	Probability
Alta Vista	1.360	0.186
Excite	0.948	0.352
InfoSeek	3.228	0.004
Lycos	3.172	0.004
Magellan	5.326	0.000
Open Text	1.005	0.325
WebCrawler	4.548	0.000
WWW Worm	2.842	0.009

$p < .05$

serious problem even when many relevant items were retrieved (see Table 5 for duplicate summary).

Most-Relevant-Item Score (MRI)

This score measured each engines' ability to present the most relevant item first. Because the score was assigned by the location of the item, lower scores represented better performance. For the reference questions, search engines' scores ranged from 3.3 to 5.3, with Open Text as the winner, followed by Excite and Alta Vista. Search engines did slightly better with the subject questions. Their scores ranged from 2.5 to 4.2, with Open Text performing the best, followed by WebCrawler and InfoSeek (see Table 6). Open Text is consistently the best in presenting the most relevant item up front for searchers.

Relevancy-Ranking Score (RR)

This score measured search engines' ability to present relevant items in the first half of a search result. For the reference questions, search engines' scores ranged from 15.5% to 45.1%, with Open Text leading the way, followed by InfoSeek and Excite. For the subject questions, their scores ranged from 23% to 52.8%, with InfoSeek as the best performer, Lycos as a close second, and Excite taking the third spot (see Table 7).

TABLE 5. Average Duplicate scores for reference questions and subject questions (N_{ref} = 42, N_{sub} = 10; for Excite N_{refE} = 44, N_{subE} = 12).

Engine	Ref.Q. Duplicate (mean)	Sub. Q. Duplicate (mean)
Alta Vista	0.3	0.4
Excite	0.1	0.3
InfoSeek	0.1	0.7
Lycos	0.3	0.3
Magellan	1.1	0.7
Open Text	0.3	0.8
WebCrawler	0.3	0.5
WWW Worm	0.4	0.1

TABLE 6. Average most-relevant-item scores (MRI) for reference questions and subject questions (N_{ref} = 42, N_{sub} = 10; for Excite N_{refE} = 44, N_{subE} = 12).

Engine	Ref Q. MRI (mean)	Sub Q. MRI (mean)
Alta Vista	4.4	3.0
Excite	4.1	4.2
InfoSeek	4.6	2.9
Lycos	4.6	3.5
Magellan	4.9	3.6
Open Text	3.3	2.5
WebCrawler	4.5	2.8
WWW Worm	5.3	4.1

TABLE 7. Average relevancy-ranking scores (RR) for reference questions and subject questions (N_{ref} = 42, N_{sub} = 10; for Excite N_{refE} = 44, N_{subE} = 12).

Engine	Ref Q. RR (mean)	Sub Q. RR (mean)
Alta Vista	25.8	41.3
Excite	33.4	48.6
InfoSeek	37.9	52.8
Lycos	27.3	52.4
Magellan	21.9	48.1
Open Text	45.1	42.7
WebCrawler	28.8	47.0
WWW Worm	15.5	23.0

Overall Performance

The four variables measured aspects of search engines' retrieval power. Figure 2 summarizes precision, duplicate, and MRI scores for reference questions. The RR scores were not included because their range was much higher and could not be properly included in this figure. The best search

FIGURE 2

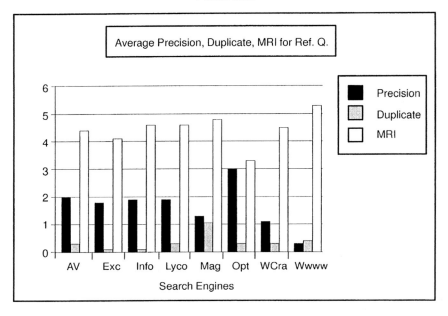

engine should have the highest precision, the lowest duplicate, the lowest MRI score and the best RR score. It is clear from Figure 2, however, that none of these search engines performed this way: Open Text had the highest precision, and the lowest MRI score, but Excite and InfoSeek had the lowest duplicates. Of the four measures, Open Text had the best scores for three of them and could be considered the best performer for this type of question. The runner-up is not as clear-cut because these engines excelled in only one or two measures. It was nonetheless possible to separate them into two groups: Alta Vista, Excite, InfoSeek, and Lycos performed relatively better than Magellan, WebCrawler and World Wide Web Worm.

Figure 3 shows a similar difficulty in identifying the winner for the subject questions. Data on Figure 3 supported InfoSeek as the best performer and the RR score reinforced that. The rest of the field was too difficult to call.

IMPLICATIONS

The search engines as a whole cover a good portion of the Internet but they were not able to produce good results for real reference questions.

FIGURE 3

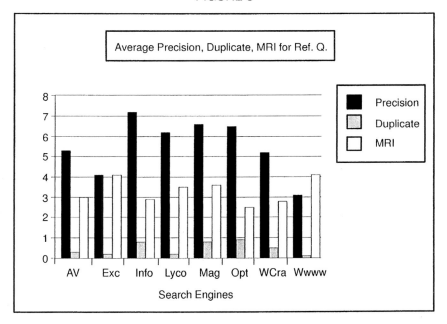

The implication here is that the Internet is not a panacea, and information seekers should not automatically turn to it for answers. Instead, they need to analyze their information needs and select information resources accordingly. Reference librarians are accustomed to this practice and they should exercise their professional judgment on the use of the Internet as well. In addition, they need to educate the public to make appropriate selection among print and electronic information resources. When online databases first became available, the public had the misconception that they contained all the answers. There is a similar misconception about the Internet, and librarians are in a good position to correct it.

The search engines, however, did well with the made-up subject questions: they had an overall average precision score of 5.6 (out of 10), suggesting that searchers are likely to be successful if their topics fall in areas for which there are many Internet resources. The challenge is to know what areas have been well covered by such resources. The public is not likely to invest much time on this task and will rely on librarians for guidance. To become knowledgeable, librarians can make use of subject guides and projects such as InfoFilter and CyberStacks. In addition, they can use listservs such as the "Stumpers-L" to tap into the expertise of other reference librarians. In turn, they can share their knowledge with users in training programs or online tutorials. System designers could assist users too by stating clearly what areas they have indexed most and how indexing is done. Right now the indexing information is hidden from searchers and, perhaps out of economic concerns, search services seem more interested in giving the impression that they cover many subject areas than in giving searchers a clear idea of the areas they have a lot of resources on (Taylor and Clemson, 1996). Perhaps as the competition rages on, these services will realize that such information can work to their advantage.

The four variables of this study indicate, to a reasonable extent, the strengths and limitations of current search engines. Users can select the variable that is most important to them and select the engine that performs best in that aspect. They may also take all variables into account and select an all-around performer such as InfoSeek for subject searches.

The low duplicate scores suggest that the problem is now negligible even in vast databases such as Alta Vista and Lycos. The relevance ranking results of the search engines are acceptable, though not spectacular. What these scores could not reveal is the frustration users experienced when they tried to understand why some irrelevant items were listed at the top of a search result. Even though two words could be specified in a search statement, some engines rank by the occurrence of single words and present items with the most occurrence of single words first. For instance, one may search for "personal finance" and specify that both terms have to be in a page for it to be retrieved, but pages with most occurrence of "personal" would be listed before pages with both words. What this did to searchers is to undermine their confidence in a search engine's relevancy ranking system. Search services could improve by explaining briefly how their ranking is done. This information does reveal the weakness of their ranking system, but searchers will have a better idea on how to view the search output.

Another issue brought up by the study is the need for new variables to measure search engines' performance. "Precision" and "Recall," the standard information retrieval measures, have to be modified or dropped. Using the top ten items as the base, searchers of this study had to follow potentially 4,680 Web pages to evaluate their relevancy. If the base were increased to thirty or fifty, the time and manpower involved in relevance assessment will increase sharply. Standard recall measure can be modified into a "relative recall" measure if researchers pool all relevant items retrieved by all the searches and use them as a base to calculate the relative recall score. The MRI variable focuses on the most relevant item retrieved, and the RR variable on a larger part of the search result; both were found adequate in measuring relevancy ranking.

CONCLUSIONS

The study evaluated eight major search engines by searching twenty-six questions twice in each of them (four times in Excite). Data show that the selected search engines could not produce good results for real reference questions but did well with made-up subject questions. It also found that search engines performed differently for the two types of questions: Info-Seek performed best with subject questions, while Open Text was best with the reference questions. The study found duplicates not to be a problem. By introducing the MRI variable and the RR variable, the study illustrates how search engines' relevancy ranking can be evaluated. By presenting data on the four variables, the study sheds light on several aspects of search engines' performance.

The study is not without its limitations. First, its data captured fleeting moments on the Internet. They offered snapshots of how the search engines worked from April to June of 1996, and the pictures may not be quite the same any longer because the Internet is expanding rapidly. Nevertheless, like Leighton's study, this one found InfoSeek to be one of the best search engines. If this research is replicated and the same findings are produced, however, one will be able to place more confidence in the findings. Second, the reference questions were collected from one academic library, and it is difficult to determine if they were representative of reference questions. Again, replication of the study would lend more credence to the findings. Third, the number of test questions probably could be increased, although this study did use more questions than most of the other studies.

On the positive side, this study introduced new variables to evaluate relevancy ranking, used a research design to compare search engines' performance for the two types of questions, advanced understanding of the performance of search engines, offered recommendations on how system designers could improve their systems, and pointed out how librarians could prepare themselves and the public for Internet exploration.

REFERENCES

All-in-one search page. [Online]. Available HTTP: http://www.albany.net/allinone/

Argus Clearinghouse. (1996). Subject guides. [Formerly Clearinghouse for subject-oriented internet resource guides]. [Online]. Available HTTP: http://www. clearinghouse.net/

Boyce, Bert R., Meadow, Charles T., & Kraft, Donald H. (1994). *Measurement in Information Science.* San Diego: Academic Press.

Brinkley, Monica, & Burke, Mary. (1995). Information retrieval from the Internet: An evaluation of the tools. *Internet Research: Electronic Networking Applications and Policy, 5* (3), 3-10.

BUBL Information Service. BUBL WWW subject tree–arranged by Universal Decimal Classification. [Online]. Available HTTP: http://www.bubl.bath.ac.uk/BUBL/Tree.html

Campbell, Karen. (1996). Understanding and comparing Web search tools. [Online]. Available HTTP: http://www.hamline.edu/library/links/comparisons.html

Courtois, Martin P., Baer, William M., & Stark, Marcella. (1995). Cool tools for searching the Web. *Online, 19* (6), 14-32.

Desai, Bipin C. (1995). Test: Internet indexing systems vs list of known urls. [Online]. Available HTTP: http://www.cs.concordia.ca/~faculty/bcdesai/test=of=index=systems.html

InfoFilter. [Online]. Available HTTP: http://www.kcpl.lib.mo.us/infofilter.htm

Internet Solutions. (1996). Internet statistics–estimated. [Online]. Available HTTP: http://www.internetsol.com/netbin/internetstats

Kimmel, Stacey. (1996). Robot-generated databases on the World Wide Web. *Database* 19 (1): 40-49.

Koster, Martijn. (1995). Robots in the Web: threat or treat? [Online]. Available HTTP: http://web.nexor.co.uk/mak/doc/robots/threat-or-treat.html

Leighton, H. Vernon. (1995). World Wide Web indexes: A study. [Online]. Available HTTP: http://www.winona.msus.edu/services-f/library-f/webind.htm

Library of Congress. WWW by subject or keyword. [Online]. Available HTTP: http://lcweb.loc.gov/global/search.html#www

Liu, Jian. (1996). Understanding WWW search tools. [Online]. Available HTTP: http://www.indiana.edu/~librcsd/search/

Lottor, Mark. (1996). Domain survey. [Online]. Available HTTP: http://www.nw.com/

McKiernan, Gerry. CyberStacks(sm). [Online]. Available HTTP: http://www.public.iastate.edu/~CYBERSTACKS/

Meghabghab, Dania Bilal, & Meghabghab, George V. (1996). Information retrieval in cyberspace. In *The Digital Revolution: Proceedings of the ASIS Mid-Year Meeting, San Diego, California May 18-22, 1996* (pp. 224-237). Medford, New Jersey: Information Today.

Netscape. Net Search. [Online]. Available HTTP: http://home.netscape.com/home/internet-search.html

Online Computer Library Center. InterCat. [Online]. Available HTTP: http://www.oclc.org:6990

Online Computer Library Center. NetFirst. [Online]. Available HTTP: http://www.oclc.org/oclc/netfirst/netfirst.htm

Packer, Joan G., & Tomaiuolo, Nicholas G. (1996). Qualitative analysis of five

WWW "search engines." [Online]. Available HTTP: http://neal.ctstateu.edu:2001/htdocs/websearch.html

Prosise, Jeff. (1996). Crawling the Web. *PC Magazine, 15* (13), 277-278.

SAVVYSEARCH. [Online]. Available HTTP: http://cage.colostate.edu:1969

STUMPERS-L. [Online.] Available e-mail: STUMPERS-L@crf.cuis.edu Also available HTTP: http://www.cuis.edu/~stumpers/intro.html

Taylor, Arlene G., & Clemson, Patrice. (1996). Access to networked documents: Catalogs? search engines? or both? *Proceedings of OCLC Internet Cataloging Project Colloquium, Jan. 1996, San Antonio.* [Online]. Available HTTP: http://www.oclc.org/oclc/man/collq/taylor.htm

Venditto, Gus. (1996). Search engine showdown. *Internet World, 7* (5), 79-86.

Webster, Kathleen, & Kathryn Paul. (1995). Beyond surfing: Tools and techniques for searching the Web. [Online]. Available HTTP: http://magi.com/~mmelick/it96jan.htm

Winship, Ian. (1995). World Wide Web searching tools, an evaluation. [Online]. Available HTTP: http://www.bubl.bath.ac.uk/BUBL/1Winship.html

APPENDIX A

Reference Questions and Subject Questions

Searchers were told to interpret "book," "books," "research," "information," etc., in these requests as "Web pages."

Reference Questions:

1. What is the correct title of the book that is the guide to manuscripts? (The patron meant [some items on] manuscript collections.)

2. What is the name of the work room in a monastery where the common work of the office is done (e.g., copying, collating papers, faxing)? [We need to find Web sites that describe the structure of monasteries.]

3. What database in ALADIN should I be looking in to see if Catholic University owns these journals? (The patron had a list of journals to check.)

4. Research on assimilation of Cuban Americans.

5. Research on television viewing and aggression in children.

6. Do you have any criticism of the play by Federico Garcia Lorca called "La Casa de Bernarda [Alba]"?

7. I need some books about Michelangelo.

APPENDIX A (continued)

8. I want to compare a preventative welfare policy with a policy which corrects the problem after it occurs.

9. Is there an apostrophe in "Funk and Wagnall's"? I am citing it.

10. Does your library have any information on play therapy?

11. I am looking for some books that criticize Dante's *Inferno*.

12. Research on jobs overseas.

13. Research on Greek and Roman mythology.

14. Looking for biographical information on Bob Wills (country musician).

15. Can you tell me if this book (the patron had a book in hand), published in 1923 by a publishing company which may be defunct, is in the public domain? [Search for Books in Print on the Web.]

16. Do you have an [know] English translation of "Las meninas"?

17. Information on education in Taiwan.

18. Information on speed limit restrictions from the point of view of keeping the speed limit at 55/65 due to accidents, deaths, etc.

19. Does the library own the papers of John Tracy Ellis? [i.e., find Web sites on this person.]

20. Can you tell me if you have any books about Irish board games? [i.e., Find Web sites on this topic.]. Fidchell is the game I am looking for [i.e., find Web sites on this game.]

Subject Questions

1. Please find some information related to Star Trek Voyager.

2. Is there any Web information on how stress related to workers' productivity?

3. People often complain that politics is dirty. Is there information on ethics in politics?

4. Is there information on how to manage personal finance or investment?

5. What is the nature of Parkinson's disease, how does the disease progress, and what are the treatment options? Any info on these topics will be helpful.

APPENDIX B

Instruction on Searching the Search Engines

🍎 *Which parts of the search engines should be searched?*

- Alta Vista: Use "simple query" for all searches. Use " " for phrase search.

- Excite: Search all queries as "concept" and as "keyword" to determine if these two search methods retrieve different items.

- InfoSeek: Search the queries in the World Wide Web file. Do phrase searches when necessary–using " " for phrase search.

- Lycos: Use the "Enhance your search" option to search for desired match. Leave the other options intact.

- Magellan: Use the standard setup. No modification necessary.

- Open Text: Use the standard setup. No modification necessary.

- WebCrawler: Use the standard setup, but you need to change the output to 10 items. Specify *all* words that should be in a page for it to be retrieved.

- WWW Worm: conduct all searches in "ALL URL References", choose the "AND" operator, and limit the search output to "50 items."

Visual Maps of the World Wide Web: Helping the User Find the Way

Ruth A. Palmquist
Susan P. Sokoll

SUMMARY. The difficulties of finding intellectual content in the multidimensional environment of the Internet pose new problems for the LIS professionals and for the users they seek to serve. Many Internet users report the "lost in cyberspace" phenomenon and print publishing has flourished surrounding users' need to find good intellectual content on the World Wide Web. This paper examines the cognitive aspects of arrangement and organization on the Internet and then examines some of the techniques being used to create maps of the intellectual content found there. Through many centuries, maps have been a helpful cognitive aid in providing a practical congruence between a large, three dimensional landscape and a portable, intuitive, two dimensional reference source. Some of the same features of maps are being used to provide some cognitive sense of the contents of special topical areas on the Internet and particularly the World Wide Web. *[Article copies available for a fee from The Haworth Document Delivery Service: 1-800-342-9678. E-mail address: getinfo@ haworth.com]*

Mental models are particularly important to users' success in navigating through information resources in computer-mediated environments.

Ruth A. Palmquist is Assistant Professor, and Susan P. Sokoll is a doctoral student, both at the Graduate School of Library and Information Science, The University of Texas, SZB 564 D7000, Austin, TX 78712.

[Haworth co-indexing entry note]: "Visual Maps of the World Wide Web: Helping the User Find the Way." Palmquist, Ruth A., and Susan P. Sokoll. Co-published simultaneously in *The Reference Librarian* (The Haworth Press, Inc.) No. 60, 1998, pp. 49-60; and: *Electronic Resources: Use and User Behavior* (ed: Hemalata Iyer) The Haworth Press, Inc., 1998, pp. 49-60. Single or multiple copies of this article are available for a fee from The Haworth Document Delivery Service [1-800-342-9678, 9:00 a.m. - 5:00 p.m. (EST). E-mail address: getinfo@haworth.com].

49

The user can come to an information system with several possible models in mind. There is the model of the work that the user needs to complete along with his or her cognitive framework of underlying knowledge, spatial and verbal abilities. There is the model of what the system can provide together with the model that the user has of how his or her interaction with the system will proceed. These later models usually draw upon the user's previous experience with the system or with similar systems. In the case of computer-mediated search and retrieval systems, prior computer experience (Koohang and Byrd 1988; Jacobson and Fusani 1992) seems to strongly affect the user's cognitive model of the system.

To improve the user's ability to use a computer based system, software developers have long known that providing mental models for the user can improve the interaction that the user has with the system. In general, a useful approach is to provide sufficient information about what the system can do and what it contains (now called meta-information or meta-data) so that the user's own cognitive strengths can be accommodated or "bootstrapped," allowing the user to draw from experience and capitalize upon his or her understanding to successfully complete an information retrieval task. In an overview of interface styles, Lindeman (1991) states that "as the reality that can be manipulated by the user gets more complex, it becomes even more important that interface designers communicate a cogent model of that reality" (p. 3). Interface designers think of these models as advance organizers–a concept coming from classroom teaching when the teacher provides a brief overview of new material to be learned thus providing learners with a way of organizing the new knowledge along with what they already know. Lansdale and Ormerod (1994) provide a particularly strong user-centered review of interface design.

The advent of the Internet and its most recent manifestation, the World Wide Web, present a multitude of possibilities to experiment with just such mental modeling. Often called meta-information modeling, a successful interaction with the user will be one that presents and arranges information in ways that are useful to the understandings or previously held mental models of the user. On the Web, hyperlinks exist to connect related items on separate pages, unrelated items of text, or even different media (audio, video, etc.), freeing the information content developer from the confines of a linear structure. Narratives are no longer bound to the page-by-page sequential unraveling of a book. Instead, the reading experience on the Web imitates the reading of a newspaper, which provide jumps between narrative parts with interruptions for other items, advertisements, or cartoons. The reader is freed, as well, from the societal constraints of a more linear text and must exist in a discontinuous space (Landow 1992).

While the explosion of the Internet, and particularly the World Wide Web (WWW), provides this freedom from narrative context, the freedom proves more problematic for the development of the user's mental modeling of the organization of material. Hyperlinks can be used almost limitlessly within a script but the discontinuity causes the reader to become lost in the maze of links. This freedom may appear exhilarating initially, but when the reader is forced to retrace his or her steps to find that critical information found twelve screens back, a level of discontent begins to build. When one jumps to a Web address, there are frequently no clear navigational clues as to how the material contained on the Web page is arranged. Some sites do provide outlines of the main divisions of their information but this does not provide the same guidance given by a book's table of contents with its division of pages among listed topics.

ORGANIZATION OF INFORMATION

Libraries, as repositories of information, have long been involved with establishing and utilizing various methods of organizing material. Information systems, whether based on paper records or on newer media, may involve physical attributes of the material itself, information content, or some combination of the two. To facilitate storage, especially of odd sized items (maps, charts, videocassette, etc.), the library may segregate items by format or type before utilizing some other method of organization. Systems of organization may focus on content, as do the familiar Library of Congress and Dewey Decimal classification systems, may be alphabetic by author (the usual arrangement for fiction books) or by title (possible arrangement of media like videocassettes), or there can be other devised systems (for example, an arrangement of genealogy books by geographic region of origin). Each of these provides the user with an organizational framework from which to locate material of a particular type.

While these systems may provide some attempt at adequate intellectual access through their systematic classification and cross-referencing, the Internet provides us with a greater challenge and a greater opportunity. The actual physical location of the item is of little concern except for its relationship to the content of other items. Often these items may be in disparate physical locations, provide widely different levels of coverage, and have varying degrees of ephemereality to the user's information search. Attempts to provide mappings of intellectual content on the Web thus far have generally resorted to lists which contain a plenitude of cross-references to areas of related interest. One has only to examine the many newsstand magazines that attempt to help users of the Web locate material of interest to see these lists employed. Other than the organization imposed by the publisher of the list itself and some indication as to the publisher's rating of the content, the user has little information on actual depth of coverage and is apt to get lost in the astonishing maze of hyperlinks that are provided once they examine the actual content of the Web.

Libraries, it has been noted, are not at the forefront of organizational efforts aimed at managing the information space of the Web. The efforts that have been proposed by and for the LIS community use the familiar descriptions of intellectual content usually provided by the MARC record, the card catalog or OPAC (Steinberg 1996). Yahoo!, originally begun by a couple of students from Stanford University, has developed a Web search service that provides a classified index to the Web. This index seems to be reinventing classifications established by libraries, albeit with broader cross-referencing and more detailed and rapidly changing classifications for new subjects. Yet the information provided by Yahoo! is nothing more than a much revised list of subjects (with hyperlinked cross references) much like an overall listing of the Library of Congress or Dewey Decimal schedules might similarly provide.

Other search engines provide nothing more helpful to understanding the meta-information structures of an indexed subject area on the Web than a ranked listing of "hits" that can then be explored by the user one at a time. These "hits," based often upon the frequency of a search term in the text of the selected Web pages, often include several references to different pages from the same site, if that site itself is highly relevant. Often these sites include cross-references to other relevant sites, giving the searcher more material to try to assimilate and organize. While this seemingly haphazard method of search and retrieval may provide some answer to the user's initial question, it still leaves the searcher with no clear idea of the scope and coverage of material he has not viewed or how extensive the sites he has seen actually are.

VISUALIZATION OF INFORMATION

The Web and the Internet not only provide an immense and growing collection of resources, they also provide the capacity to utilize various kinds of visual modeling techniques. Thus far in Internet history, the majority of these visualization techniques have been provided by the more thoughtfully created sites with accompanying visual pointers to specific subject matter the site contains. However, visualization can and has been used to provide access to information as easily and often more effectively than print (Tufte 1983).

Metaphors are a method that humans use to understand abstract or complex subjects. They are frequently used to describe emotions, states of being, and political actions. They have also been used extensively in the design of computer interfaces. Macintosh appropriated the desktop metaphor (which was then used by Windows) to describe functions that could be performed on the computer (i.e., file folder, trashcan). Various broad types of metaphors have been evolved to describe access to the Internet as an understandable entity. However, there is little evidence that a "best" metaphor exists (Palmquist 1996).

Metaphors are most effective when they are easily understood by the users, when they present a series of common elements which can be used in metaphor construction, and when they map fairly closely from the source to the target domain (Madsen 1994). The variety of metaphors that have been used to describe the activity on and resources of the Internet provides researchers with fertile ground from which to evaluate usage, applicability, and user understanding, assimilation and use. Construction of additional references utilizing the same base metaphor strengthens the framework and makes the metaphor stronger. A recent example of this strengthening of the metaphor can be seen in current AT&T advertising. "Surfing the Web" has long been a popular metaphorical expression for the fluid navigational decisions one can make while on the Internet. Current AT&T ads picture business men and women, dressed for a day at the office, standing next to their surf boards. No real explanation of the surf boards is given in the ad, so the underlying strength of the "surfing" metaphor must carry the sense of the ad. Without a broad recognition of that metaphor by the population the ad seeks to reach, the combination of Wall Street, business attire, and the surf boards would seem quite incongruous.

While many of the metaphors used for the Internet are strong in the number of references that can be generated and in some degree of general agreement among users as to the appropriateness of the metaphor to its particular reference, the issue of users' understanding must be considered in terms greater than that of western culture. While metaphors using surfing or frontiers or spiders may seem appropriate to Americans, they may lack the cultural basis for understanding by non-western societies. One of the most powerful metaphors for the Internet is that of travel/navigation. While much has been made of the "information superhighway," the road metaphor can be understood by most cultures in the world, and navigation, in the sense of moving purposefully from one point to another, is another powerful construct. This metaphor can easily expand to encompass the use of facilities like Yahoo! or other search engines as the cartographic tools like maps or indexes available to the would-be navigator/traveler.

The most effective method of presenting spatial information has been the map (Wood 1992). The map is a multicultural creation which has existed for centuries in various guises and forms. It provides a metaphoric reference to the existing world from a series of carefully designated points and relationships. Maps provide a referential framework which allows the user to gain access to information at varying levels. Location of one place can easily be established, but a map can also be used to find other places in relation to that one. It can also establish a collection of places to similar size, geographic orientation, and many other classificatory types. Maps generally provide spatial orientation to a physical dimension, although they can be used to show a relationship between imaginary places as well (i.e., a map of Dante's inferno or Tolkien's ring series).

There is a substantial body of research on the benefits of maps as devices which aid the cognitive understanding of physical space. One of the best studies demonstrating the benefits in quickly orienting the user was done by Bartram (1980). In that study, subjects were presented with information about bus routes in four different ways: as a road map; as a schematic map; as a list of bus stops in sequential order; and as a set of lists of bus stop names in alphabetical order. Subjects' knowledge of the bus routes were tested using a series of logical IF-THEN inference problems. The study found that the bus route information represented by schematic map generated the fastest decision making results, and the information presented by alphabetical list generated the slowest decision results, particularly when the inferences involved highly complex information.

Maps are also important in that they exist across cultural boundaries. While the cartographic conventions that denote a typical map from the U.S. Geological Survey may not be completely understood by everyone, the basic function of a map as a navigational tool is understood.

MAPPING THE INTERNET

There have been several attempts in the last three years to provide a mapping of Internet sites in a non-virtual format. These maps appear to have been produced for the novice user of the Internet, and were sold bundled with a computer magazine. The format for these items retained the traditional accordion pleated, tri-folded appearance of the typical street map.

The first of these maps was provided in the spring of 1994 in an issue of

PC Computing. The content is loosely organized in the broad categories of business, finance and economics, reference and education, government and technology. While this scheme appears rather limited in its scope, the map was devised specifically to introduce non-users or novices to the Internet. Subscribers to *PC Computing*, a magazine designed for general users, are more likely to come from non-technical business positions than those in computer-related fields (who probably would have already experienced the Internet). The emphasis placed in the map on business, finance, and technology mirrors the sites which might be of most interest to these subscribers.

The categories are designated by using various colors and are arranged across the map as radiating out from nodes (red balls of varying sizes). These nodes are specific sites for which the Internet address (URL: Uniform Resource Locator) is provided and the nodes are cross-linked to each other. A brief, written description of each site's content is provided along the connecting links between nodes. The map itself contains no real geographic information and often does not seem to cognitively attempt any classification of the aggregations of information within the broader categories, but instead appears to provide a smattering of items that obviously appealed to the editors of the magazine. The sites provided are scattered across the map in a random fashion with no apparent order. Government sites are positioned with universities and sites in different countries are located beside each other. While the primary node is given a URL address, the information provided on the radiating lines, which often represents nothing more than links to another site, remain without any locational information.

The map does exhibit several other features that are more associated with a traditional road map—the familiar grid (A-M, 1-12) with a printed alphabetical index to the sites and slight variations in background color to suggest the existence of land and water. However, these various references to land and water appear more to provide some cartographic verisimilitude than to provide any useful locational assistance.

Following the lead established by *PC Computing* to provide this random agglomeration of interesting sites, other maps emerged for those Internet users who might be seeking underground sites, musical sites, etc. Each of these retained the familiar road map features as a adjunct to give users the editors' favorite Internet locations.

PC Computing introduced yet another Internet map in the summer issue of 1996. While this similar tri-folded format again retained the road map format it was really more of a wall chart divided by various types of Internet operation. Users are provided with a short list of various types of

Internet sites, such as search engines, gophers, etc. A URL is provided for each location. Here the mapping function becomes nothing more than a convenient method of packaging material. The map provides no linkages other than the categories established for the lists. The map is also nothing more than an actual paper list which is replicated virtually at numerous Internet locations. The paper map is a very poorly conceived artifact that is not even thorough in its designation of categories of sites. The visual nature of the map is completely subsumed in the provided lists and text.

While the potential remains for a visual representation of the Internet by subject area, the paper maps produced thus far have not lived up to their cartographic tradition. A map provides the user with a relationship between items listed. Although this relationship has been spatial in most maps produced thus far, there is no reason why the metaphor of mapping cannot be used to represent information in some other method.

RECENT MAPPINGS OF THE INTERNET

The need for visual representation of intellectual organization and depth of coverage can be met by use of maps designed to provide alternate organizational structures to the ever expanding variety of lists. Several attempts have been made recently to provide visually defined access to the Internet.

A small preliminary study that attempts to answer the question "What constitutes a landmark in hypertext?" was conducted at the School of Library and Information Science, Indiana University (Heffron, Dillon, and Mostafa 1996). Subjects were given the opportunity to recall characteristics about a hypertext search experience. These "characteristics" were operationalized as those features that appeared on the screen during the subjects' search for a specific piece of information. Given up to 10 minutes for the specific task, subjects were then asked to recall the details of what they did during the search. To highlight the "lost in cyberspace" effect, researchers found that the path they had identified, approximately seven links, became far longer at the hands of the subjects (anywhere from 20 to 30 links at the highest). In terms of remembered details, four out of seven subjects claimed they could not remember any features on the screens that had seen. Of the remainder, subjects generally remembered the entity that had created the page (Yahoo! search screen, school's home page, etc.) rather than salient features of those pages. Researchers intend to do further work and did suggest that the difficulty of articulating screen features may be part of the subjects' difficulty.

A group of researchers at the Technical University of Helsinki, utilizing the self-organizing mapping (SOM) technique of T. Kohonen (1995), have provided a visual display of the postings to various newsgroups (URL: http//websom.hut.fi). Here the intellectual content is represented in relationship to that of the other newsgroups by physical location on the screen. The depth of coverage in the particular intellectual area is visually provided by varying shades of color, from white (least coverage) to red (intense coverage).

The snapshot nature of this project is merely to show how a SOM could be used to provide a visual mapping of Internet sites preserving intellectual relationships as well as indications of coverage. The hyperlinks on the map provide the viewer with descriptions of what was included in the particular category and do not attempt to provide access to the actual material used in the construction of the site since this was a test of how SOM could be applied to the Internet.

One limitation to the use of SOM is that the selection of features to be modeled must be provided prior to using the algorithm. This requires that a great deal of pre-processing preparation come before presenting a map to the user. Yet the algorithm, given the properly prepared data within the features selected, can produce relational maps which provide as well some indication of the depth of coverage in the content.

Another use of SOM in portraying Internet content can be found at a site at the University of Kentucky. The URL for this site implies its intent (http://lislin.gws.uky.edu/Sitemap/Sitemap.html). Using Java and the Kohonen SOM algorithm, several mappings have been constructed of five sites on the Internet. The mappings again show the size of the subject area through the size devoted to it on the map. Intellectual proximity of items is noted by their proximity to each other on the map. This relationship is determined by the frequency of occurrence of key words in each of several fields.

A third project using SOM has been conducted under the guidance of Hsinchun Chen at the University of Arizona (http://ai.bpa.arizona.edu/ent). This site, designated *ET-SPACE,* provides a visual guide to entertainment servers and homepages (over 110,000 were surveyed). The site contains a clickable SOM and a searchable thesaurus both of which were generated automatically. There are two layers of maps, one containing the overall mapping of sites, and secondary maps available below the initial map. These secondary maps are derived from the initial mapping from closely proximate areas with more than 100 URLs.

A different effort of mapping uses the more familiar notion of co-citation analysis. Larson (1996) provides an exploratory study of 115 Web pages of material in the earth sciences. The pages were initially collected using the Web search engine Inktomi "WebCrawler." Once the core set of Web pages concerning earth science were identified, the Alta vista search engine (http://www.altavista.digital.com) provided by Digital Equipment Company was used to gather data on the strength of co-citations existing between all pairings of these 115 sites. Using an advanced search feature of Alta Vista, two sites can be paired and a list of the sites that point to both members of the pair can be identified. To accomplish this task, Alta Vista provides an advanced search feature called link. The link feature, together with a Boolean logic connector, allows the user to type an expression like "link:pubweb.parc.xerox.com/map AND link:xtreme.gsfc.nasa.gov." The result of this query will be a list of all sites that contain links to both of the original sites. The resulting list can be interpreted as a co-citation value of the relatedness of the original pair. Larson then used the co-citation value for his various pairings to map the dissimilarity between sites within the earth sciences specialization. He did this using the multi-dimensional scaling statistical approach available in SAS as the ALSCAL procedure. The resulting plot is a two-dimensional mapping of the relationships between the various sites within a discipline. The more often two sites are linked together from a third site, the stronger the similarity between them is believed to be. This approach has been used in bibliometrics to determine the relationship between major works in a specialization, but this was a novel use of the co-citation approach to the mapping of a Web-based specialization.

FUTURE OF VISUALIZATION OF THE INTERNET

Visualization techniques hold great promise for helping users build mental models of portions of the Internet. Metaphors have the ability to communicate large complex notions with a simple icon or phrase. Maps and other visualization techniques, like metaphors, create the possibility of communicating large amounts of information to the user with a single glance at an map or icon. Mapping also provides a means of access to Internet intellectual content in a manner more visual than a list. A map can depict both simple relationships and more complex classificatory details that may guide the user in selecting appropriate areas of the Web for initiating a search or for a more unfocused browsing effort. Maps can be built in layered sequences providing ever increasing complexity or depth of content for a particular subject area.

Self-organizing maps or SOMs provide one approach to visualization that already has many supporters in the computer science community. Self-organizing maps were inspired by biology. They use a complex network of computational relationships to model the distance between two resources on the Web by defining the distance between them (much like the aforementioned co-citation measure of dissimilarity) by calculating the shortest path or number of links. The process does not depend on any prior knowledge of the data and therefore is described as self-organizing. The computations were originally used to model the sort of biological processes that learn to self-organize, like the motor nervous system. SOMs provide several necessary talents for dealing with the vastness of the Web. They could be used to depict a very small area of Internet content, but they are scalable to depict very large content areas as well. Some of the SOMs that have been developed (see http://heiwww.unige.ch/girardin/cgv/www5) make use of hyperlinks as clickable points within the mapping to provide the user with the ability to move easily from the map to a particular site, thus increasing content identification as well as actual access. SOMs could be used to provide an overall mapping of a particular Web site or be scaled to provide access to a large variety of Web sites composed on a particular intellectual theme or content focus. A university's website could provide access not only to its departments (often done in a listed arrangement only) but to the intellectual components that lie within them. Thus a mapping could show a close relationship between geography and anthropology, or between communication and library and information science, and so forth. This large mapping could then contain links to more detailed maps created to display the relationships of the subjects within a particular discipline. A sub-map of law would provide access to torts, constitutional law, copyright, etc. Each of these could then be broken into their component parts and so on, until each field of study is analyzed and visually presented through layers of maps.

Visualization techniques can be used to provide a different type of access to intellectual content of the Internet than has been previously used by libraries and information agencies. SOMs are only one possible family of such techniques. The co-citation mapping that has long been done in bibliometrics seem also to hold promise for showing graphically the intellectual connections between Web sites on a similar topic. The computing power available over the Internet and the visual resources that can be used allow us to experiment with a variety of organizational methods and approaches to information. As librarians we have the understanding of the complexity of the subjects and a good understanding of the users and their tasks; now we must experiment to make multidimensional information space more navigable for users. Only by trying can we advance beyond the confines of the traditional "list" and the somewhat restrictive relationships captured through the MARC record or card catalog approach.

REFERENCES

Bartram, D.J. (1980) "Comprehending Spatial Information: The Relative Efficiency of Different Methods of Presenting Information about Bus Routes." *Journal of Applied Psychology* Vol. 65. p. 103-110.

Girardin, Luc. (1996) "Mapping the virtual geography of the World Wide Web." <URL:http://heiwww.unige.ch/girardin/cgv/www5/>.

Heffron, J.K., Dillon, A., & Mostafa, J. "Landmarks in the World Wide Web: A Preliminary Study." In: Hardin, S. (ed.) *Global Complexity: Information, Chaos and Control–Proceedings of the 59th Annual Meeting of the American Society for Information Science* Vol. 33: p. 143-145.

Jacobson, T. & Fusani, D. (1992) "Computer, System, and Subject Knowledge in Novice Searching of a Full-Text, Multifile Database." *Library and Information Science Research* Vol. 14: p. 97-106.

Koohang, A.A. & Byrd, D.M. (1987) A Study of Attitudes Toward the Usefulness of the Library Computer System and Selected Variables: A Further Study. *Library and Information Science Research* 9(2): 105-111.

Kohonen, T. (1995). *Self-organizing maps.* New York: Springer-Verlag.

Landow, G. P. (1992). *Hypertext: the convergence of contemporary critical theory and technology* Baltimore, Md.: Johns Hopkins University Press.

Lansdale, M. W. & Ormerod, T. C. (1994) *Understanding interfaces: A Handbook of human computer dialogue* London: Academic Press.

Larson, R. (1996) "Bibliometrics of the World Wide Web: An Exploratory Analysis of the Intellectual Structure of Cyberspace." In: Hardin, S. (ed.) *Global Complexity: Information, Chaos and Control–Proceedings of the 59th Annual Meeting of the American Society for Information Science* Vol. 33: p. 71-78.

Lindeman, M. J. (1991) "Interface styles." In: Dillon, M. (ed.) *Interfaces for information retrieval and online systems: The state of the art.* New York: Greenwood Press, p. 3-9.

Madsen, K. H. (1994). "A guide to metaphorical design." *Communications of the ACM* 37(12): 57-62.

Palmquist, R. A. (1996). "The Search for an Internet Metaphor: A Comparison of Literatures." In: Hardin, S. (ed.) *Global Complexity: Information, Chaos and Control–Proceedings of the 59th Annual Meeting of the American Society for Information Science* Vol. 33: p. 198-202.

Steinberg, S. G. (1996). "Indexing the Web: Who are these Yahoos, anyway?" *Wired* 3(5): p. 108-182.

Tufte, E.R. (1983). *The Visual display of quantitative information.* Chesire, Conn: Graphics Press.

Wood, D. (1992). *The Power of maps.* New York: Guilford Press.

Search Tactics of Web Users in Searching for Texts, Graphics, Known Items and Subjects: A Search Simulation Study

Ingrid Hsieh-Yee

SUMMARY. This study examines the search tactics used by Web users to start their searches and deal with search problems such as too many postings and no relevant postings. Four search topics were developed to allow for comparison of search tactics used in four types of searches. The tactics analyzed include search statements, number of search statements, starting points, and tactics to solve the two search problems mentioned above. Search statements were searched in Alta Vista to determine their success and their nature was analyzed. With regard to the tactics used to address search problems, t-tests and chi-square tests found no difference between searches for texts and searches for graphic information, and between known-item searches and subject searches. Some of Web users' search tactics were similar to those for online searching or online catalog searches, but several tactics were unique to Web searching. *[Article copies available for a fee from The Haworth Document Delivery Service: 1-800-342-9678. E-mail address: getinfo@haworth.com]*

Ingrid Hsieh-Yee is Associate Professor, School of Library and Information Science, Catholic University of America, Washington, D.C. 20064. E-mail: hsiehyee@cua.edu

The author would like to thank Ms. Harriet Nelson, the Head of Reference Services of the John K. Mullen of Denver Memorial Library, and her staff for their assistance with data collection.

This project was supported by a research grant from the Catholic University of America.

[Haworth co-indexing entry note]: "Search Tactics of Web Users in Searching for Texts, Graphics, Known Items and Subjects: A Search Simulation Study." Hsieh-Yee, Ingrid. Co-published simultaneously in *The Reference Librarian* (The Haworth Press, Inc.) No. 60, 1998, pp. 61-85; and: *Electronic Resources: Use and User Behavior* (ed: Hemalata Iyer) The Haworth Press, Inc., 1998, pp. 61-85. Single or multiple copies of this article are available for a fee from The Haworth Document Delivery Service [1-800-342-9678, 9:00 a.m. - 5:00 p.m. (EST). E-mail address: getinfo@haworth.com].

INTRODUCTION

Just how large the World Wide Web and the Internet are, no one really knows, except that they are huge. The July report by Lottor (1996) estimated that the Internet will double its size in twelve to eighteen months, suggesting that at least twice as much information will be available by the end of 1997. That means the need to organize Internet resources is more urgent than before. How can we have a clear idea what information is available, where it is kept, and how to get to it? Search tools have evolved from Archie, Gopher and Hytelnet to search engines and indexes for the World Wide Web. These tools were designed to help searchers find what they need; and yet, there is little evidence that the use and search behavior of non-technical users was taken into account–the original, awkward commands of Archie attests to this problem. Such a development may have something to do with the fact that earlier Internet users were fairly adept at using computer technology, so designers did not have to be too concerned about the issue of user-friendliness.

The arrival of the World Wide Web and its popularity brought about by Mosaic in 1993 and Netscape in 1994 have greatly changed the backgrounds of Internet users. Their technical knowledge is not as solid as that of the earlier groups, and demand for user-friendly tools will intensify. It is true that the Web's multimedia and hyperlink capabilities have made Web surfing fun and exciting; and users now can gopher, telnet, ftp, and follow newsgroup threads from the World Wide Web. But that does not mean that users are very successful in finding what they need. Search engines and robots were developed and used to set up search services because they can automatically roam the Internet and index some parts of it. But the issues of user-friendly interface, effective retrieval, search assistance continue to be secondary in many search services.

It is true that search engines and Web indexes are easier to use than Archie or Veronica. And yet, users are also finding it more and more difficult to be knowledgeable about the features of so many search engines and to choose the right tool–*PC Computing*'s map for searching the Web (1996), for instance, serves to underscore such challenges. Here again we have many tools, especially search engines, designed to help users but created with little user input. In this model, users are expected to learn the tools and express their needs in ways the tools can process.

Since resources are being added to the World Wide Web at an exponential rate and more users around the world will be participating in the Web, search tools will be required to be more user-friendly than before, and Web information will have to be properly organized. Instead of letting designers develop new search tools and ways to organize information, we need to start with the users by understanding how they search for information and how they deal with search problems. It is only with such knowledge that we can design tools and organize information in ways that will facilitate their normal ways of searching. It was with this goal in mind that the present study was undertaken.

LITERATURE REVIEW

Demographic and use data on Internet users have been reported (Pitkow & Recker, 1994, 1995; Bishop, 1994; Pitkow & Kehoe, 1996), but the search tactics and strategies of Web users remain to be investigated. Catledge and Pitkow's research on client-side user events of NCSA's Mosaic (1995) was probably the first study of Web users' navigation strategies. Analyzing log files, they found that users typically had no idea of the location of Web documents and relied on hyperlinks or other heuristics to navigate to a specific document. They also identified three types of browsers: serendipitous browser, general purpose browser, and searcher. Data revealed a "spoke and hub" search pattern showing users moving no more than two layers in the hypertext structure before returning to the entry point. The study was somewhat limited because it lacked the context for collected data. It was similar to viewing the transaction logs of an online catalog to detect search patterns without knowing why a search was conducted. The study nevertheless provided intriguing findings and should stimulate more research in this area.

Search behavior, search strategies and search tactics have received much attention from researchers in library and information science. Fenichel (1981) provided an excellent survey on factors affecting search process, and Bates (1981) presented an overview of search techniques and theories. Bates was the first to point out that a search tactic is a move used to further a search, while search strategy refers to a search plan for an entire search (1979a). She presented seventeen "idea tactics" that can help searchers generate new ideas or solutions to search problems, and identified twenty-nine "search tactics" to move a search along (1979a, 1979b). The search tactics are defined in four categories: monitoring, file structure, search formulation and term tactics. Fidel (1985) analyzed about eighty searches and identified eighteen operational moves that do not change the meaning of query components and twelve conceptual moves that change the meaning of those components. These concepts of idea tactics, search tactics, and search moves provide a theoretical framework for several studies. Analyzing documents librarians' service, McClure and Hernon concluded that idea tactics and search tactics could be used to improve documents reference service (1983). In comparing search strategies for documents and general reference, Moody also found Bates' tactics promising in improving search success (1991). Hsieh-Yee (1993) operationalized several of Bates' search tactics in analyzing how search experience and subject knowledge affect the use of search tactics. She found search experience affected the use of many search tactics and that subject knowledge became a factor only after searchers have had a certain amount of search experience. Wildemuth, Jacob, Fullington, de Bliek, and Friedman (1991) used Bates' search tactics and Fidel's search moves to categorize end users' searches of a microbiology database. They found "Browse/ Specify," "Select," "Exhaust," "Intersect," and "Vary" to be the most common moves and that "selection of moves varied by student and by problem" (p. 302). Wildemuth, de Bliek, He, and Friedman (1992) analyzed over 200 searches for search moves of novice searchers and found them using a small number of moves. They also found their definitions of move valid in classifying end users of a factual database. Along a similar vein, Shute and Smith (1993) identified thirteen knowledge-based search tactics which were used by search intermediaries to help searchers with search problems; and the tactics are very similar to those identified by Bates. In addition, search tactics have also been used to develop new information systems. Smith, Shute, Caldes, and Chignell (1989) used the knowledge-based tactics to build an experimental semantically-based search system, EP-X; and Buckland has incorporated search tactics to design OASIS, a prototype adaptive online catalog (1992). Search tactics and search moves have been operationalized somewhat differently in the studies above, but it is clear that these tactics have been used to deal with three typical problems in information searching: when too many items are retrieved, when too few items are retrieved, and when nothing relevant is retrieved. The present study made use of this framework and several of Bates's search tactics and Fidel's search moves to examine Web users' search for information.

RESEARCH QUESTIONS

Instead of collecting aggregate search data without any context, this study investigated users' tactics when they searched for four different types of information. The study was designed to answer the following research questions:

- What are searchers' tactics in searching for a known item which is text-based?

- What are searchers' tactics in searching for a known item which is graphic-based?
- Are the tactics used for these two types of searches different?
- What are searchers' tactics in searching for known items?
- What are searchers' tactics in searching for subjects?
- Are the tactics used for known-item searches and subject searches different?

METHODOLOGY

A repeated measurement design was used to collect data. Four search requests were developed and forty Internet users were recruited. Since a large number of students at the Catholic University of America are novice Internet users, the investigator decided a search simulation exercise would be more productive than actual search exercises. In this design users would not need to be proficient with the search features of a search tool or the interface of a browser. Furthermore, because the search problems are hypothetical and controlled, users could describe their tactics for these problems in a more consistent manner than they could in real searches. It is understood that in this design Bates' search tactics for monitoring and file structure were not likely to be used. Nevertheless, tactics for search formulation and term selection may still be observed. Users' tactics would indicate what they would do to solve search problems. They represent what users *intended to do*, and may or may not be the same as their online tactics for similar search problems.

Selection of Web pages. The graphic capabilities of the World Wide Web make it attractive to users, but it was not clear whether users searched for graphic information differently from how they searched for textual information. To address this question, the investigator identified two Web pages for the experiment: one is a strategic paper which is text-based, the other a Web page of photos, therefore graphic-based (see Appendix A). The original plan to include a Web page that was entirely graphic and contained no textual information was abandoned because pretests found it too difficult for users to formulate a search statement. Both Web pages contain a long title, an author, and corporate bodies.

To contrast tactics for known-item searches and subject searches, the investigator derived two subject searches from the chosen Web pages. The experiment therefore included four search requests:

1. To search for a text-based known-item, "The Presidential decision directive on multilateral peace operations."

2. To search for Web pages similar to the previous item.
3. To search for a graphic-based known-item, "Survivors: a new vision for endangered wildlife."
4. To search for Web pages similar to the "Survivors" page.

Each study instrument contained these requests and the requests were rotated so that order effects, if any, would be equally distributed. Twenty subjects received a study instrument that listed the requests in the above order, while the other twenty subjects another study instrument that listed requests for the "Survivors" page first.

Subject selection and data collection. Posters for the study were posted around the Catholic University of America and interested participants were directed to the reference desk at the main library. Library science students were excluded from the study. Each participant received a study instrument and the instruction to turn it in before leaving the library. No time limit was imposed and participants could work on the study instrument anywhere in the library (most of them chose to do it at the reference area). Each subject was paid five dollars for his or her participation. Data collection began in April and concluded in May 1996.

Data analysis. Forty responses were received, but three were incomplete and excluded from final analysis. Dependent variables examined in this study are search tactics used when a user began a search (the starting point and the search statements), the number of search statements, the tactics used when too many items were found, and the tactics used when nothing relevant was found. Bates's tactics for addressing these search problems, as illustrated in a 1987 paper, Fidel's search moves (1985), and the definitions validated by Wildemuth, de Bliek et al. (1992) were consulted in categorizing users' moves.

In addition, users' search statements were searched against Alta Vista to determine their success in retrieving desired items. Alta Vista was chosen because it has indexed more than 30 million Web pages and provides access to Web pages, newsgroups, ftp files, and other Internet resources. Previous studies analyzed search statements or queries by checking how well the statements matched subject headings (e.g., Bates, 1977; Connell, 1991; McJunkin, 1995), but that was not feasible in this study because search engines index different information spaces of the Internet and do not use controlled vocabulary for indexing purposes.

Knowing numerous search statements would be given for the known items, the investigator had decided to focus on the first search statements. For the subject searches, users were asked to provide two statements, and both statements were checked against Alta Vista. As for the tactics in dealing with search problems, the analysis focused on the first tactics used for both problematic situations. Responses were categorized and counted. For nominal data chi-square tests were performed to determine the relationship between variables; for numerical data t-tests were performed.

FINDINGS

Background of Participants

All participants were students at the Catholic University of America and about two-thirds of them were undergraduates. Most respondents were not heavy users of the Web: sixty-two percent used the World Wide Web for no more than two hours a week (see Table 1). Their total number of hours in using the Web was also relatively low: sixty-seven percent had used the Web for no more than seventy-five hours (see Table 2). Seventy-three percent usually searched the Web by Netscape, but ninety-seven percent have tried graphic browsers in exploring the Web.

TABLE 1. Respondents' Hours of Web Searches per Week (N = 37)

Hours	Number	Percent
Under 1 hour	11	30
1-2 hours	12	32
3-6 hours	9	24
7-10 hours	4	11
More than 10 hours	1	3
Total	37	100

TABLE 2. Respondents' Total Hours of Web Experience (N = 37)

Hours	Number	Percent
Less than 50 hours	12	32
50-75 hours	13	35
76-100 hours	5	14
More than 100 hrs.	7	19
Total	37	100

Analysis of Search Statements

Alta Vista searches. For the known-item searches, respondents' first search statements were checked against Alta Vista to determine if they could retrieve the known items. Because the search results could be very big, it was decided that the evaluation would be based on the first ten items retrieved–this practice was used by Leighton (1995) and Packer and Tomaiuolo (1996). As Table 3 shows, search statements for the "Survivors page" (graphic-based) had better success than those for the "Presidential page" (text-based). But in subject searches, respondents' search statements for the Presidential page were more successful than their statements for the Survivors page. It is also worth noting that respondents used a hierarchical approach–searching by parent organizations–to retrieve the known Presidential page and pages similar to it, but did not use this approach as frequently in searching for the Survivors page or pages similar to it.

Nature of access points. Both known items contain information on author, title, and corporate bodies, but respondents' use of these potential access points was very different (see Table 4). Twelve respondents searched the Survivors page by James Balog, the photographer, five by its full title, and these searches were successful. But no respondents searched for the Presidential page by its author, William Lewis, and only one respondent searched it by its full title. One respondent was not able to

TABLE 3. Search Success in Alta Vista and the Use of the Hierarchical Approach

Searches	Success (%)	Failure (%)	No response	Total*	Hierarchical approach (%)
Known-item searches (N_k = 37)					
Presidential page	18 (49%)	19 (51%)	0	37	18 (49%)
Survivors page	25 (68%)	12 (32%)	0	37	0 (0%)
Subject searches (N_s = 74)					
Presidential page	59 (80%)	10 (14%)	5	74	13 (18%)
Survivors page	46 (62%)	22 (30%)	6	74	2 (3%)

*For the known-item searches only the first search statements were searched against Alta Vista. For the subject searches respondents' two statements were searched.

TABLE 4. First Search Statements Used to Search for the Known Items (N_k = 37)

Statements	Survivors page			Presidential page		
	Number	Success	Failure	Number	Success	Failure
Author	12	12	0	0	0	0
Full title	5	5	0	1	1	0
Partial author	1	0	1	0	0	0
Partial title	18	8	10	10	7	3
Corporate Bodies[a]						
Parent body 1	0	0	0	8	0	8
Parent body 2	0	0	0	8	8	0
Parent body 3	NA	NA	NA	2	0	2
Keywords	1	0	1	8	2	6
Total	37	25	12	37	18	19

[a]The Survivors page includes Photo Perspective which is the host of this Web page and Harry N. Abrams, Inc., the publisher, but neither of these was used by respondents. The three corporate bodies for the Presidential page include the National Defense University, its Institute for National Strategic Studies, and the Institute's Strategic Forum; all of them were used by respondents.

retrieve the Survivors page by the photographer's last name alone while eighteen respondents used partial titles with mixed success. In contrast, most of the ten respondents searching for the Presidential page by partial title were successful.

Corporate bodies are not known to be the type of access points frequently used by catalog users for known-item searches; instead, author and title have been reported to be the favorites (Lewis, 1987). Users' searches for the Survivors page certainly fit this traditional pattern. But their searches of the Presidential page suggest another approach that is encouraged by the World Wide Web structure–the hierarchical approach. Because Web pages can be, and often are, moved around easily, Internet users sometimes find a given URL (Uniform Resource Locator) no longer able to bring up the desired Web page. One of the common solutions is to go to the host site, which is usually the parent organization, and follow the organizational structure there to find the new location of a Web page. Similarly, Internet users sometimes enter a partial URL to reach a subdirectory, which could be considered a mid-level corporate body, and determine where a desired Web page has been placed. Such practices might have contributed to respondents' decision to take the hierarchical approach to the Presidential page: eighteen respondents used corporate bodies, including eight for the top-level body ("National Defense University"), eight for the mid-level body ("Institute for National Strategic Studies"), and two for the lower-level body ("Strategic Forum"). In contrast, no corporate bodies were used to search for the Survivors page. The hierarchical approach, however, was not always successful (see Table 4).

Keywords taken from the text of the known Web pages were not used as frequently as the other access points when respondents searched for known items. These search statements proved to be of little use in retrieving these pages.

Of the 74 first search statements given for the known items, 31 (42%) failed. The failure could be attributed to a number of reasons. Indexing limitations, for instance, could explain some of the problems. Several respondents looked for the Survivors page by the title proper, "survivors." This attempt would have worked well in online catalogs, but Alta Vista was not able to retrieve this page and present it among the first ten because (a) its indexing is done by keyword, (b) there are many Web pages containing the word "survivors," and (c) Alta Vista does not allow for searching by the title field. This problem became worse when searchers chose a common word such as "wildlife." They may have assumed that because this word was part of the title, the page would be retrieved. They did not realize however that the large number of Web pages containing this word would push the Survivors page way back and they would have to browse many items to get to it.

Inadequate provision of hypertext links and incorrect assumptions on the searchers' part could account for problems with using some corporate bodies. For instance, by using "National Defense University" (NDU) a searcher assumed that there would be links to guide them to the desired Web page, but no such links were provided at the NDU site. Similarly, when searchers tried "Strategic Forum" they expected to see the desired Web page listed as a link because the Web page is about one of the strategic forums. And yet, such a link was not provided.

Subject searches for pages similar to the known pages turned out to be more successful than the known-item searches. Respondents relied on keywords in the known pages and synonyms they could think of and were fairly successful. Thirty-two of the 137 statements failed (23% failure rate), and the main reason was that search terms were too broad. Instead of searching for "endangered wildlife," respondents used "animals," "wildlife" or "environment." A related reason was the use of "form" in searching for graphic information. Unlike items represented in library catalogs, which usually index their forms, Web pages were indexed by their words. So if a Web page contains photos but does not specifically include the word "photographs," a searcher will not be able to retrieve it by the that word. Similarly, there are no standard expressions for forms, so someone searching for "pictures" will not be able to retrieve Web pages that contain picture but use the word "photos" in their pages. A very small percent of searchers included a "form" component in their search statements.

The hierarchial approach for subject searches deserves our attention because it is so different from typical subject searches in online catalogs. Thirteen respondents searched for pages similar to the known pages by corporate bodies associated with them, and they were successful. This could be because these corporate bodies do have specific subject focus, and they also provide links to Web pages on related topics. The lesson here is that the hierarchical approach can be useful for subject searches, as long as relevant links are provided from them. This is a capability of the World Wide Web that is most appealing and potentially most useful. The provision of appropriate links depends on the designers of Web pages; a quick review of Web pages found that, except in the entertainment areas, links have been underprovided in many Web pages.

Analysis of Search Tactics

Types of starting point. For all four search requests participants were given five choices of starting points to choose from. As Table 5 shows, "search engine" was the most popular starting point (93 responses, 63%), followed by "commercial service provider" (26 responses, 18%). Many respondents named Netscape as the commercial service provider and indicated they would start their searches there, implying they would use the "Net Search" feature of Netscape to get to a search engine. It is therefore reasonable to conclude that the number of students starting with a search engine is probably higher than sixty-three percent.

It is also worth noting that in searching for the Presidential page and pages similar to it, twelve respondents said they would start with a "university site." What they meant by that is they would start with the site of "National Defense University" which is the corporate parent of the given Web page. This approach suggests that Web users seemed to have a better grasp of the concept of parent organization and were willing to take a hierarchical approach to seeking information.

Tactics used when too many items were retrieved. This problem was phrased slightly differently for known-item and subject searches, but the questions essentially asked for the same thing, i.e., tactics searchers would

TABLE 5. Starting Points for Known-Item and Subject Searches by Types of Information Sought

Types	Known-item searches (N_k = 37)			Subject searches (N_s = 74)			TOTAL (N_ks = 148)		
	Text	Graphic	Subtotal	Text	Graphic	Subtotal	Text	Graphic	Total
Library site	2	4	6	2	4	6	4	8	12
University site	7	1	8	5	3	8	12	4	16
Search engine	21	25	46	24	23	47	45	48	93
Commercial	5	8	13	6	7	13	11	15	26
No answer	1	0	1	0	0	0	1	0	1
Total	36	38	74	37	37	74	73	75	148

use when many items were retrieved. "Browsing" the search result was the most popular answer across the four searches (66, 45%, see Table 6), followed by moves to narrow the search, including adding another term to the first search statement or using a more specific term for searching (58, 39%). Trying a different search term or a synonym was the next popular choice, reported by twenty (14%) of the respondents.

Tactics used when nothing relevant was retrieved. Reported tactics could be grouped into ten categories. "Using another term" was the most common tactic (45, 30%, see Table 7), followed by "using a different search engine" (33, 22%) and "asking for help from librarians or others or check other library tools" (17, 12%). The third category probably could be attributed to respondents' relative inexperience with the Internet, but it also underscored novice Web users' need for human intervention and more traditional mode of assistance.

The range of tactics used in this problematic situation may seem unsystematic at first, but it serves to contrast the similarities and differences between searching library catalogs or databases and searching the World Wide Web. For instance, change of search engines, selecting items for possible hyperlinks, and checking the Web site of a parent organization are tactics unique to the World Wide Web. But broadening a search with more general terms, narrowing a search with more specific terms, trying related subject categories, and using synonyms are tactics applicable in online catalogs and databases. This group of common tactics, however, also reveals the incongruence between users' expectations and search engines' indexing practices. By the use of controlled vocabulary and cross references, online catalogs offer searchers a network of indexing terms (broader, narrower, related, and synonymous terms), and Web users seemed to expect the same kind of network to be working on the World Wide Web, not knowing that so far no search engines have provided such a conceptual network for their index terms.

Comparison of Search Tactics in Searching for Texts and Graphic Information

To determine whether searchers used different tactics to search for textual information and graphic information, chi-square tests were performed when the dependent variable is a nominal variable, and t-tests were performed when the dependent variable is an interval variable. These tests were conducted for known-item searches and for subject searches. The significance level of all tests was set at the .05 level. The independent variables were the types of information sought and the dependent variables included "START" (types of starting points), "MORE"

TABLE 6. Tactics Used When Too Many Items Were Retrieved

Tactics	Known-item searches (N$_k$ = 37)			Subject searches (N$_s$ = 74)			TOTAL (N$_{ks}$ = 148)		
	Text	Graphic	Subtotal	Text	Graphic	Subtotal	Text	Graphic	Total
Browse the result	15	15	30	17	19	36	32	34	66
Select a few items to follow their links	0	0	0	1	1	2	1	1	2
Narrow the search by adding another term or search by a specific term	15	15	30	15	13	28	30	28	58
Use a different search engine	1	1	2	0	0	0	1	1	2
Try another term or a synonym	5	7	12	4	4	8	9	11	20
Total	36	38	74	37	37	74	73	75	148

TABLE 7. Tactics Used for Dealing with Zero Hits

Tactics	Known-item searches (N_k = 37)			Subject searches (N_s = 74)			TOTAL (N_ks = 148)		
	Text	Graphic	Subtotal	Text	Graphic	Subtotal	Text	Graphic	Total
Browse	0	2	2	0	2	2	0	4	4
Select a few items to view	2	3	5	0	2	2	2	5	7
Narrow the search	3	3	6	4	3	7	7	6	13
Use a different search engine	9	7	16	8	9	17	17	16	33
Look for related subjects	1	1	2	0	1	1	1	2	3
Broaden search statement	3	3	6	5	5	10	8	8	16
Use another term or synonyms	10	12	22	13	10	23	23	22	45
No answer	1	1	2	2	0	2	3	1	4
Ask for help from librarians or others	5	5	10	3	4	7	8	9	17
Check parent site	2	1	3	2	1	3	4	2	6
Total	36	38	74	37	37	74	73	75	148

(tactics for too many item retrieved), and "NONE" (tactics for no relevant item retrieved). All chi-square test statistics indicated that no significant relationship between the independent variables and the dependent variables has been determined to exist. In all chi-square tests more than 20% of the cells had frequency less than 5, so one needs to treat these results with caution. Nevertheless, since the level of test significance was set according to the restrictions specified for extreme departure from the ideal of equal expected frequencies (Roscoe, 1975), it was assumed that the test results could be accepted. Table 8 summarizes the test results.

Number of search statements identified for known-item searches. The search statements respondents would use to search for the known items were also analyzed according to the nature of the Web page sought. For the Presidential page the number of statements given ranged from 1 to 13, with a mean of 5.944. For the Survivors page the number of statements ranged from 1 to 32, with a mean of 5.868. T-test statistic ($t = .080$, $df = 72$, $p = .937$) shows that no significant difference could be found in the number of search statements used for searching the two types of information.

Taken together, six chi-square tests and one t-test indicate that in searching for texts and graphic information searchers did not use different

TABLE 8. Chi-Square Tests of Search Tactics Used for Searching Textual Information and for Graphical Information

	Texts vs. Graphics		
Tactics	Chi-Square	DF	Prob.
	Known-item searches		
START	7.158	4	.128
MORE	.279	3	.964
NONE	2.913	9	.968
	Subject searches		
START	1.265	3	.737
MORE	.254	3	.968
NONE	8.069	9	.527

$p < .05$

number of search statements or different types of search tactics in dealing with their search problems.

Comparison of Known-Item Searches and Subject Searches

To determine whether searchers used different tactics for searching known items and subjects, three chi-square tests were performed. Following the restrictions specified by Roscoe (1975), the test significance was set at the .05 level for all tests. All three test statistics indicated that no significant relationship between the independent variable (types of searches) and the dependent variables (the three groups of tactics) has been determined to exist. Table 9 summarizes the test results.

Overall Pattern of Search Tactics

Patterns of search tactics emerged when search tactics used for all four questions were compared. As Table 10 shows, respondents tended to use the same starting point for their searches. For the two known-item

TABLE 9. Chi-Square Tests of Search Tactics Used for Known-Item Searches and for Subject Searches

Known-item vs. Subject searches

Tactics	Chi-Square	DF	Prob.
START	1.011	4	.908
MORE	5.414	4	.247
NONE	3.278	9	.952

$p < .05$

TABLE 10. Similarity of Search Tactics Used for Various Searches

Tactics	Known-item searches		Subject searches		All 4 searches	
	Same	Different	Same	Different	Same	Different
START	27	10	33	4	25	12
MORE	23	14	20	17	10	27
NONE	21	16	16	21	10	27

searches, twenty-seven of the thirty-seven respondents (73%) used the same starting point; for the two subject searches, thirty-three (89%) did so; and twenty-five (68%) did so for all four searches. The same tendency could be observed with "MORE," the group of tactics for dealing with the problem of having too many items: twenty-three used the same tactic when they searched for known items; twenty did so when they conducted subject searches; and 10 did so for all searches. A similar pattern for the "NONE," the group of tactics for dealing with the problem of not retrieving relevant items, can be detected from Table 10 as well. There are six respondents whose tactics for START, MORE, and NONE remained consistent for all four searches. To determine whether such a pattern of behavior was associated with their hours of Web searches per week or their total hours of Web experience, two chi-square tests were performed, with the test significance set at the .05 level. Test statistics show no significant relationship between the search pattern and respondents' experience or time with the Web could be found.

DISCUSSION

In terms of the search statements used to search for the Survivors page and the Presidential page, Web users showed distinct differences. On the Survivors page the graphic part includes words and images. Title appears on top, followed by author, other graphic, then the corporate body which presents the photos. Author and title information is presented again with more text information on the lower part of the page. Twenty-four of the thirty-seven users (65%) circled components of the graphic part as their search statements to retrieve this page. From the graphic and text information users must know (and were assumed to know) that this page represents graphic information (photos), but in their searches, they chose conventional access points such as author or title. This could be because users knew that search engines would not allow searching by graphics, or it could be that words are easier than graphics for humans to communicate. Hastings showed how difficult it was for art historians to describe images (1995); and it might not be surprising that users would rely on words whenever possible.

In contrast, eighteen of the thirty-seven users (49%) searched for the Presidential page by the corporate bodies. Such a difference could be attributed to users' greater reliance on parent organizations when searching for Internet resources. Or it could be that because the corporate bodies were more prominently presented than the author, these users mistook them as the authors. If this theory of prominence were true, one would expect "Strategic Forum," the most prominently listed corporate body of the three, to be used most. Data show, however, that it was the least used among the three. It is therefore probably safe to conclude that the tactic of using higher corporate bodies (or host sites) was at work here. What these findings suggest is that the nature of a Web page, be it text or image, probably will not affect how people look for them if typical elements such as author and title are present on a page. Future studies could use a Web page that is entirely graphic with no caption or text information accompanying it to explore how users search for it. They may also examine the use of corporate bodies for known-item searches on the World Wide Web to verify the use of the hierarchical approach among Web users.

Although the Survivors page is about images, very few users conducted subject searches for this type of information by form. This again suggests that the nature of a Web page was not affecting searchers' tactics. Most of the subject searches were successful (71%) and users showed a strong reliance on keywords; but a small number of them chose to search by corporate bodies, suggesting users' expectation that these bodies would offer information similar to the given pages. One common problem for search failure was the use of concepts that were too broad. The success of keywords for subject searches deserves a few comments. Granted, they were able to retrieve some relevant items, but they also included many false drops. Perhaps the usefulness of keyword searching depends largely on the purpose of a search. For a quick, cursory search, keyword searching is promising even on the Web; but for more in-depth or extensive searches, the limitations of keyword searching, such as the lack of control over synonyms and the need for context to make the words more specific, will result in many irrelevant items for the searcher to wade through. The need for controlled vocabulary has been voiced by librarians and library and information science researchers (e.g., Taylor and Clemson, 1996), but no search services, except OCLC's NetFirst, have implemented it. If the market demand becomes stronger however, search services may comply with users' wishes.

Users' tactics in solving search problems showed that regardless of the types of searches or the form of the information sought users will deal with search problems in similar manner. When too many items were retrieved, users were not daunted by the huge retrieval. Rather, they were willing to sift through many items to find what they needed. One explanation could be that most search engines present retrieval results in a succinct format, making it possible for users to browse the results quickly and easily. But browsing does not guarantee the answer. The heavy reliance of users on browsing indicates the ineffectiveness of search engines' filtering system. Search engines have been slow in incorporating filtering features such as proximity operator, field-specific search, set combination, limiting by non-subject parameters (time, place, format), and online thesaurus. The newest search engine, HotBot, allows users to limit their search by date, media type, and location. Perhaps others will soon follow suit.

As for the problem of retrieving no relevant items, users dealt with it in the same way regardless of the types of searches or the form of the information sought. The three most popular tactics suggest that users were aware of the difficulty in searching the Web. Their use of another search term or a synonym indicates their knowledge that the burden is on them to think of possible search terms. Those preferring to change search engines show that they knew search engines produce different search results. And those seeking help from others or turning to library catalogs and other tools suggest that a lack of confidence and a willingness to rely on a more traditional approach for information seeking.

By knowing Web users' search tactics, system designers could improve their system accordingly. They could add more filtering features and improve the presentation of the first search result so that browsing can be easily done. Users mentioned the use of synonyms, specific terms, narrower terms, and broader terms, thereby revealing their expectation (or misunderstanding) that such a network is already in place in the databases of the search engines. If the search engines are to have a future, they will have to make their searches easier. Furthermore, as information is being added to the Web rapidly and very soon search engines will soon realize that keyword searching will no longer be adequate for retrieval. A good alternative is to use controlled vocabulary and let users take advantage of the linkage between indexed terms.

Librarians could use the findings to design training programs. Users should be instructed to know the database size, the indexing policies, the relevancy ranking algorithm, and the subject areas on which an engine has a lot of data so that they can search more efficiently. Assuming that the information retrieval on the Web will not change much in the near future, librarians should develop heuristics to help users. One of the most important contributions librarians can make for information retrieval on the Internet is to demonstrate how users and search engines alike can benefit from controlled vocabulary. They could, and should if given the opportunity, also assist search services in incorporating controlled vocabulary into their systems.

CONCLUSIONS

This study investigated how users searched for text and graphic information, how they searched for known items and topics, and how they dealt with search difficulties. The study instrument was a search simulation exercise and participants were recruited from one university campus. Because of these limitations, the findings can not be generalized to real search exercises or a larger population. Nevertheless, the study shed light on the use of search tactics, identified search tactics unique to Web searches, and discussed how search services, system designers and librarians could help to make information retrieval on the Web easier for users. The findings also provide future research possibilities. Researchers could analyze search tactics used in real Web searches and compare them with our findings. As more and more graphic information is added to the Web, they could examine how users search for graphic information. They could investigate if the hierarchical approach is commonly used in Web searching. The heuristics and strategies used by librarians and users to cope with the limitations of current information retrieval on the Web is another area for investigation. But most important of all, research is needed to assist us in determining to what extent the theories and practices of information retrieval can be applied to networked information.

REFERENCES

Bates, Marcia J. (1977). Factors affecting subject catalog search success. *Journal of the American Society for Information Science, 28*, 161-169.
Bates, Marcia J. (1979a). Idea tactics. *Journal of the American Society for Information Science, 30*, 280-289.
Bates, Marcia J. (1979b). Information search tactics. *Journal of the American Society for Information Science, 30*, 205-214.
Bates, Marcia J. (1981). Search techniques. *Annual Review of Information Science and Technology, 16*, 139-169.
Bates, Marcia J. (1987). How to use information search tactics online. *Online, 11* (3), 47-54.
Bishop, Ann P. (1994). A pilot user study of the Blacksburg electronic village. In *Navigating the Networks: Proceedings of the ASIS Mid-Year Meeting, Portland, Oregon, May 21-25, 1994* (pp. 18-42). Medford, New Jersey: Learned Information.
Catledge, Lara D., & Pitkow, James E. (1995). Characterizing browsing strategies in the World-Wide Web. *Computer Networks and ISDN Systems, 27*, 1065-1073.
Connell, Tschera Harkness. (1991). Techniques to improve subject retrieval in

online catalogs: Flexible access to elements in the bibliographic record. *Information Technology and Libraries, 10* (2), 87-98.

Fenichel, Carol Hansen. (1981). The process of searching online bibliographic databases: A review of research. *Library Research, 2* (2), 107-27.

Fidel, Raya. (1985). Moves in online searching. *Online Review, 9* (1), 61-74.

Hastings, Samantha K. (1995). Query categories in a study of intellectual access to digitized art images. In *Proceedings of the ASIS Annual Meeting, Chicago, Illinois, October 9-12, 1995* (pp. 3-8). Medford, New Jersey: Learned Information.

HotBot. (1996). [Online]. Available HTTP: http://www.hotbot.com/

Hsieh-Yee, Ingrid. (1993). Effects of search experience and subject knowledge on the search tactics of novice and experienced searchers. *Journal of the American Society for Information Science, 44*, 161-174.

Leighton, H. Vernon. (1995). World Wide Web indexes: A study. [Online]. Available HTTP: http://www.winona.msus.edu/services-f/library-f/webind.htm

Lewis, David W. (1987). Research on the use of online catalogs and its implications for library practice. *Journal of Academic Librarianship, 13* (3), 152-57.

Lottor, Mark. (1996). Domain survey. [Online]. Available HTTP: http://www.nw.com/

McClure, Charles R., & Hernon, Peter. (1983). *Improving the quality of reference service for government publications.* Chicago: American Library Association.

McJunkin, Monica Cahill. (1995). Precision and recall in title keyword searches. *Information Technology and Libraries, 14* (3), 161-171.

Moody, Marilyn K. (1991). Documents search strategies and general reference search strategies: An analysis and comparison. *Reference Librarian, 32*, 57-69.

Online Computer Library Center. NetFirst. [Online]. Available HTTP: http://www.oclc.org/oclc/netfirst/netfirst.htm

Packer, Joan G., & Tomaiuolo, Nicholas G. (1996). Qualitative analysis of five WWW "search engines." [Online]. Available HTTP: http://neal.ctstateu.edu:2001/htdocs/websearch.html

PC Computing. (1996). Map to navigating the Web. *PC Computing, 9* (8): Supplement. Contents of the map also available HTTP: http://www.zdnet.com/pccomp/lowband/webmap/spmaps/map0896/

Pitkow, James, & Recker, Mimi. (1994). Results from the first world-wide web user survey. *Computer Networks and ISDN Systems, 27*, 243-254.

Pitkow, James E., & Recker, Margaret M. (1995). Using the Web as a survey tool: Results from the second WWW user survey. *Computer Networks and ISDN Systems, 27*, 809-822.

Pitkow, James E., & Kehoe, Colleen M. (1996). Emerging trends in the WWW user population. *Communications of the ACM, 39* (6), 106-108.

Roscoe, John. (1975). *Fundamental research statistics for the behavioral sciences* (2nd ed.). New York: Holt, Rinehart and Winston.

Shute, Steven J., & Smith, Phil J. (1993). Knowledge-based search tactics. *Information Processing & Management, 29*, 29-45.

Smith, Philip J., Shute, Steven J., Caldes, Deb, & Chignell, Mark H. (1989).

Knowledge-based search tactics for an intelligent intermediary system. *ACM Transactions on Information Systems, 7,* 246-270.

Taylor, Arlene G., & Clemson, Patrice. (1996). Access to networked documents: Catalogs? search engines? or both? *Proceedings of OCLC Internet Cataloging Project Colloquium, Jan. 1996, San Antonio.* [Online]. Available HTTP: http://www.oclc.org/oclc/man/collq/taylor.htm

Wildemuth, Barbara M., Jacob, Elin K., Fullington, Angela, de Bliek, Ruth, & Friedman, Charles P. (1991). A detailed analysis of end-user search behaviors. In *ASIS '91. Systems understanding people. Proceedings of the 54th Annual Meeting of the American Society for Information Science, Volume 28, Washington, D.C., 27-31 October 1991* (pp. 302-312). Medford, New Jersey: Learned Information.

Wildemuth, Barbara M., de Bliek, Ruth, He, Shaoyi, & Friedman, Charles P. (1992). Search moves made by novice end users. In *Proceedings of the 55th Annual Meeting of the American Society for Information Science, Pittsburgh, 26-29 Oct 92* (pp. 154-161). Medford, New Jersey: Learned Information.

APPENDIX

Web pages used for known-item and subject searches

A Presidential Decision Directive
Multilateral Peace Operations

William Lewis

Workshop Conclusions

- A recent presidential decision directive contains criteria for peace operations that, if strictly applied, could result in decisions to avoid U.S. participation in nearly all military operations.

- There is a danger that the failed Somalia mission will inhibit U.S. efforts to play constructive roles in UN peace operations.

- There is a need to establish formal and ongoing consultative procedures with Congress -- possibly involving a senior consultative group -- to assure Congressional involvement prior to U.S. engagement in peace operations.

- The Directive downplays the important policy area of remedial steps for effective humanitarian assistance programs.

- Efforts to strengthen UN peacekeeping capabilities may be hampered if current UN management procedures are not reformed.

Specific Issues

During the Cold War, the United Nations could resort to multilateral peace operations only in the rare circumstance in which the interests of the Soviet Union and the West did not conflict. By 1989, both the United States and the Soviet Union perceived that such operations could serve as cost-effective tools in preventing, containing, or solving conflicts that threatened international peace and stability. In many instances, they would benefit from having to bear only a share of the burden. However, since 1989, territorial disputes, armed ethnic conflicts, civil wars, and total collapse of governmental authority in failed states have presented ongoing challenges to the institutional, financial, and operational capabilities of the UN system. The UN is currently involved in about 20 peacekeeping operations.

In 1993, President Clinton initiated a wide ranging review of factors to be considered in supporting UN peacekeeping and peace enforcement resolutions, including circumstances under which American forces will be provided and the issue of command authority over these forces. The extended review which required negotiation of division of responsibility between State and DOD, resolution of command-and-control questions, and consultation with Members of Congress was completed by Spring 1994 and approved by the President early in May. The PDD, which was little changed from the original during the review process, establishes guidelines and criteria in addressing the full range of UN activities from preventive diplomacy through traditional peacekeeping, peace enforcement, and peacebuilding. It stipulates guidelines for committing U.S. forces. (See the chart below.) U.S. participation in UN peace operations is not to substitute for U.S. capacity to fight and win its own wars in short, support for UN peace operations should not degrade overall.

Survivors: A New Vision of Endangered Wildlife is a provocative and internationally acclaimed look at endangered wildlife. It includes 37 portraits of animals whose continued existence is called into question by human manipulation of nature. Moreover, it challenges us to reach a new understanding of our presence and position on the earth.

Please read James Balog's <u>Artist's Statement</u> for a full explanation of the concepts behind this ground-breaking work. The exhibition is organized geographically by the continent(s) in which the animals roam: <u>Africa, Asia, South/Southeast Asia, Australia/South Pacific, Europe, North America,</u> and <u>South America.</u>To view a section, click on its heading.

Beside each exquisite photograph you will find data regarding each endangered animal's habitat and status, and Balog's compelling commentary. Using the navigational buttons provided on the top of each page, you can further educate yourself about <u>environmental</u> issues (Biodiversity and Animal Extinction) and environmental <u>activism</u> through a kaleidoscope of maps and charts, and a list of organizations fighting to save our environment.

Click on <u>James Balog</u> to read his biography. <u>Video A</u> and <u>Video B</u> allow you to enter Balog's photo sessions with a Grizzly Bear (A) and a Gray Wolf (B). Access the <u>Comments</u> page to send a message to James Balog or the Photo Perspectives Museum's Curators.

A print exhibition entitled *Survivors: A New Vision of Endangered Wildlife* has toured museums and galleries throughout Europe and North America. An award-winning book of the same name is published by Harry N. Abrams, Inc., New York.

GEOGRAPHIC
INFORMATION SYSTEMS

Geographic Information Systems in Library Reference Services: Development and Challenge

Lixin Yu

SUMMARY. This paper introduces Geographic Information Systems (GIS) user services in libraries. It presents the concept and functions of GIS and compares the use of GIS with library map collections. GIS project in libraries are reviewed. Different kinds of GIS user services are examined. The article looks into the challenges in adding GIS to user services in libraries. User access to GIS in libraries is discussed. It argues that simplified user interfaces and multiple levels of usage are important to improve user access to GIS. *[Article copies available for a fee from The Haworth Document Delivery Service: 1-800-342-9678. E-mail address: getinfo@haworth.com]*

Lixin Yu is Assistant Professor, School of Information Studies, Florida State University, Tallahassee, FL 32306-2100.

[Haworth co-indexing entry note]: "Geographic Information Systems in Library Reference Services: Development and Challenge." Yu, Lixin. Co-published simultaneously in *The Reference Librarian* (The Haworth Press, Inc.) No. 60, 1998, pp. 87-110; and: *Electronic Resources: Use and User Behavior* (ed: Hemalata Iyer) The Haworth Press, Inc., 1998, pp. 87-110. Single or multiple copies of this article are available for a fee from The Haworth Document Delivery Service [1-800-342-9678, 9:00 a.m. - 5:00 p.m. (EST). E-mail address: getinfo@haworth.com].

"Where" is one of the most frequently asked questions. We make spatial decisions every day. We travel for work, shopping, and recreation. Before we go to a supermarket, choose a family doctor, select a daycare center, or buy a house, we need to make decisions considering path, distance, adjacency, and other geographically related information, such as environment and neighborhood. Answering geographical questions and providing access to geographical sources are important tasks of library reference service.

Maps and atlases are major parts of library geographical sources. Librarians and users are familiar with the paper forms of map sheets and atlases. However, computer technology has "invaded" this area and is inspiring a revolution in geographic reference services and map librarianship. This technology is known as Geographic Information Systems (GIS).

GIS may still sound new to many library patrons, but it has been widely used in federal and local government agencies for urban planning, crime control, natural resource management, environmental protection, and many other applications. For example, the Office of Analysis and Evaluation at the Food and Nutrition Service (*FNS*, now called the Food and Consumer Service, *FCS*) of the U.S. Department of Agriculture started two GIS research projects in 1992. The projects used the administrative data on food stamp retailers and recipients and converted their addresses into map locations. Maps were created to demonstrate the location and annual sales of the food stamp retailers, as well as the distribution of the food stamp recipients. The result was used with mathematical models to analyze the accessibility of food stamp recipients to food stamp retailers.

GIS has also been widely used in the private sector. "A gold mine of geographic knowledge is ready to be unleashed from your company's internal data files!" (Castle, 1993) statements sound exciting. An example of a GIS application in business is direct marketing. The company's database has collective information about markets, demographic information, sales trends, competitive information and so on. It appears that people in similar neighborhoods often spend like their neighbors. GIS can manipulate this data and suggest which addressees are more likely to buy the product in the future. More and more companies have changed from "mass marketing" to "accountable advertising." The increase in sales is worth far more than the cost of GIS.

In addition to the large scale projects using GIS, individual users may also use GIS for study and research. With a colorful map showing two or more variables, scholars may obtain an insight, generate a research hypothesis, and demonstrate the result in a more vivid way. Students, from those in elementary and middle schools to graduate students, can learn how to study the world geographically. GIS not only makes their current assignments more attractive, it also makes them more creative in their careers in the future.

GIS applications in libraries are a recent innovation, not appearing until the late '80s. A literature review shows that articles specifically addressing library GIS applications were most frequently published in 1995. The following chart illustrates the number of documents in this area as indexed by two major information science abstracts–Information Science Abstracts and Library Literature (see Figure 1).

As Figure 1 shows, there is a dramatic increase of literature on GIS in libraries in 1995. Considering the fact that there is a time lag between the research and the publication of articles, library GIS projects should have taken off in 1993 or 1994. This paper will introduce the capabilities of GIS, examine what GIS services libraries provide, study users' reaction to this new technology, and suggest future studies in this area.

UNDERSTANDING GIS

GIS is mistakenly interpreted by many people as a map maker, or even an electronic map browser. Consequently, the difference between traditional map collections and digital spatial data/GIS can be wrongly understood as the relationship between paper form documents and full text databases. To clarify the confusion presented here, we need to answer questions such as what GIS is and what GIS can do.

FIGURE 1. Number of GIS/Libraries Articles Indexed by ISA and Library Literature

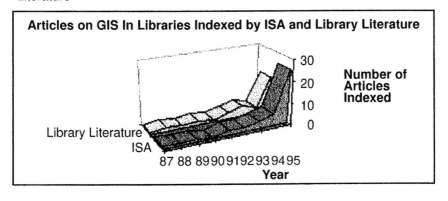

Definition of Geographic Information System

Like the concept of Information Science, GIS has as many definitions as one can imagine. One of the widely accepted definitions is "An organized collection of computer hardware, software, geographic data, and personnel designed to efficiently capture, store, update, manipulate, analyze, and display all forms of geographically referenced information" (ESRI, 1991, p. 1-3). This definition includes the components and functions of GIS.

GIS is a system that processes geographical information. There are two categories of data for GIS to manipulate. One is called *geographic data*, the shapes and locations of geographic entities. For example, the longitude and latitude of a supermarket is shown as a point; the location and shape of a street segment as a line; and the location and shape of census tract boundaries as a polygon. Another category of data is called *attribute data*, which describes the characteristics of the geographic entities. For example, the annual sales of a supermarket, the street name of a road segment, and the average income of a census tract are all attribute data. GIS uses geographic data as the major link to organize geographic referenced attribute data and to perform spatial operations on the data–this is the key feature which differentiates GIS from other information systems.

GIS Functions

If the above definition is too abstract to understand GIS, examining GIS' functions can give us a vivid picture of the system. GIS can perform various spatial operations on the data, such as calculating the distances between points and lines, reporting the length of a line or the area of a polygon, analyzing the topological relationship among points, lines and polygons, as well as conducting other more complicated analyses such as three dimensional models. A typical GIS has these functions:

. *Data Entry And Editing:* Data may be entered using a digitizer, scanner, or keyboard and mouse. When a digital street map is available, GIS can also convert street addresses (text) into map locations automatically by matching the addresses with the data in the digital map. Each GIS software has its own file format, just as Microsoft Word and WordPerfect have different file formats. Some GIS packages are able to convert files in other formats into a usable form. Typically, it takes the system a while to perform the conversion.

Part of GIS is a database management system. Users can add, delete, and edit attribute data. They can also do other database operations such as database merges. Users can also add or delete geographic entities on the map interactively.

Data Query: While the topological relationship of geographic entities is established and attributes are associated with the geographic entities, there are various ways for users to query the spatial database. Users can seek the characteristics of a location. By clicking the mouse on a map, users can find out the name of the street, the annual sales of a supermarket, or the average income of a census tract. Sometimes, users want to identify locations that meet a certain condition, such as requesting all counties whose populations are under 100,000.

GIS supports many kinds of spatial queries. Users may query the system to identify all the households within four miles from a mall; to display all the criminal cases in a zip code area, or to show all the buildings within one mile of a river. Mathematical models can be introduced to predict consequences under certain circumstances. For example, GIS can simulate a flood and indicate which area is in danger. It can also help to select the site of a new supermarket by examining factors such as the locations of competitors, transportation, population distribution, etc. Users often ask GIS to find the best way to get to one place from another. GIS can identify the shortest and the fastest ways considering factors such as the road conditions, speed limit, and distance.

Data Organization: GIS can reorganize data into different spatial units, and compare information across different features or databases. Users may put different 'maps' together to create a new map. This operation is called *overlay.* Each individual map to be overlaid is called a layer. Figure 2 illustrates an overlay process.

The second layer in Figure 2 represents a park, where a town plans to build a theater. The park council decides not to build the theater within 300 meters of the river. The first layer in Figure 2 is a 600 meter wide buffer area along the river. In Figure 2, GIS performs an overlay to erase the river buffer area from the park. The theater can be built in the shaded area in the third layer. GIS can also overlay points, lines, or polygons on polygons. Users may keep map features in all layers, or use one layer as a 'cookie cutter' to get a part of another layer. These kinds of analysis are beyond the capabilities of other database management systems.

Data Output: Maps are the most popular output of GIS. GIS users can select the variables to map, data ranges, and map scale. Many GIS users see presentation mapping as the major use of GIS. Presentation maps can be used to show the locations of different features and activities. Maps that show the attributes of features are called thematic maps. The attributes can be displayed using different colors, patterns, shapes, and sizes. For example, users may select dark blue to represent areas where average annual income is below $15,000. They may use thicker lines to represent high-

FIGURE 2. Overlay Process

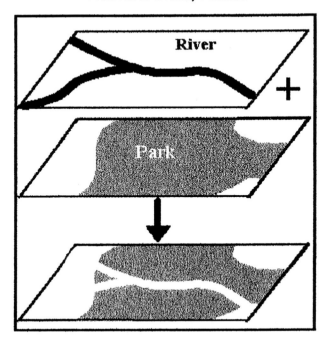

ways. Squares can be used to represent supermarkets while triangles can be used for restaurants. The size of the square may represent the annual sales of each supermarket. Figure 3 is an example of a thematic map.

Maps are not the only output of GIS. Users can also get tabular data from GIS analysis. For example, a database marketing agency can use GIS to create a list of addresses for mailings. Currently, most library users see maps as the only GIS product. Few use GIS in libraries to perform complicated analysis.

DIFFERENCES BETWEEN TRADITIONAL MAPS AND GIS

Maps are traditionally understood as published maps and atlases. The most obvious difference between maps and GIS is the difference in media–maps are in paper form while GIS involves digital data. However, the real difference is in philosophy: paper maps are static in nature, while GIS is dynamic. Paper maps are printed, unchangeable. They can be indexed

FIGURE 3. Thematic Map – Population Growth in Atlanta

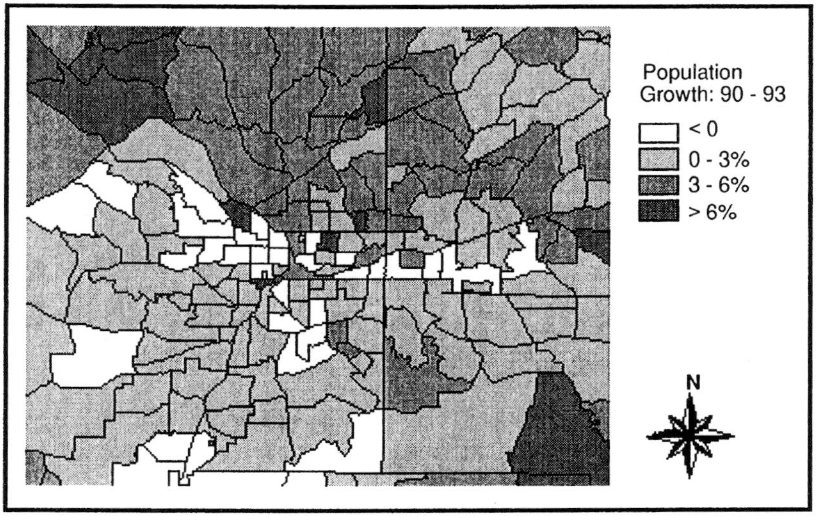

Population
Growth: 90 - 93
☐ < 0
▨ 0 - 3%
▩ 3 - 6%
■ > 6%

N

and retrieved. Paper map users need to find the map which fits their needs most closely. Compare this to GIS: clients are GIS users and map creators. They use GIS software to organize and manipulate data, choose variables and scales, make data ranges, and create customized maps which fit their needs directly. Lai and Gillies stated that the primary difference between a traditional spatial data library and a GIS data library is the higher level of selectivity and the separation of the information from the paper medium (Lai and Gillies, 1991). Lang identified this as "the very nature of GIS–its ability to integrate information on the fly to create new maps" (Lang, 1992, p. 883). This is a process of creating new information rather than simply retrieving existing information. Given a database containing 50 attributes, such as income and crime rate, if a user wants to create a map with two attributes displayed to study the correlation, he has $C_{50,2} = 1,225$ possible combinations to choose from!

Marble concluded that maps have the following limitations: (1) hard to retrieve large numbers of map elements; (2) hard to determine the complex relationships in a quantitative fashion; (3) hard to overlay maps for analysis; (4) expensive and time consuming to update (Marble, 1984). These limitations illustrate the advantages of GIS over maps. Dangermond listed ten advantages of Geographic Information Systems (GIS), including the fast speed for data retrieval, small physical storage space required, low cost of data maintenance, and great capability of spatial analysis (Dangermond, 1990).

GIS does have its disadvantages compared with maps, especially for library use. GIS requires hardware, software, data, and personnel, and any one of the four components is expensive, especially for organizations like libraries. Additionally, patrons need extensive training to use GIS themselves, while they can use paper maps without much problem. For a user who 'fears' computers and new programs, paper maps are definitely a better choice.

GEOGRAPHIC DATA IN LIBRARIES

Topologically Integrated Geographic Encoding and Referencing (TIGER) Files

About 1,400 depository libraries receive information from the government, including the famous TIGER files. TIGER is a coast-to-coast digital map database developed by the Bureau of the Census and U.S. Geological Survey (USGS). Originally designed to support census programs and surveys, this byproduct of the 1990 Census of Population and Housing turned out to be a major data resource for GIS applications. The Census Bureau extended and updated its computerized Geographic Base File/Dual Independent Map Encoding (GBF/DIME) files, which contain digital descriptions of streets and other map features, address ranges, and ZIP codes in the urban cores of 345 metropolitan and other highly developed areas. At the same time, USGS scanned or digitized its most current 1:100,000-scale maps covering all of the nation's land area. Their mutual effort created this single, integrated geographic database for the entire U.S.

The TIGER files contain information which describes the points, lines, and areas on Census Bureau maps. The TIGER file uses a vector format, which means that all the associated information is tagged with line segments. Each "line" has a beginning point and an ending point (nodes). If the line is not straight, there will be a series of shape points (vertices) in between the nodes to make the shape. TIGER contains latitudes and longitudes of more than 28 million nodes, which form nearly 40 million line segments. The lines, in turn, can form various kinds of areas, such as census tracts.

One misunderstanding of TIGER is to consider it as a street map showing Census data for the whole nation. TIGER is a digital database that can be used to make maps and link to other Census data products, but it needs to be transformed into special formats that GIS software can use. As

Kollen and Baldwin said: "TIGER files don't DO anything for you until you translate the codes by using GIS software" (Kollen and Baldwin, 1993, p. 26). The translation can be done automatically by computer, but the process is CPU-intensive and time consuming. For example, to transform TIGER to Arc/Info format for an average sized county, it may take a 486DX33 computer five hours to complete the work.

Some libraries purchase read-to-use data from third party vendors rather than processing TIGER files themselves. Wessex and Geographic Data Technology, Inc (GDT) are both famous data vendors who supply enhanced geographic data.

Census Files and Other Attribute Data

TIGER contains information such as census tract numbers and ZIP codes. It does not contain attributes such as house value, income, age, sex, etc. All this information can be found in census files such as STF-1, STF3A, and many other individual files. This data can be linked with the spatial database and processed by GIS. Today, this data usually is available on CD-ROMs in a popular format, such as DBF or ASCII.

GIS PROJECTS IN LIBRARIES

According to Lang, the earliest GIS project in libraries was the TIGER Test project in January 1991, sponsored by Cartographic Users Advisory Council. This pilot project was designed to introduce the pre-census TIGER files to libraries. The project tested seven GIS software packages in 27 libraries in the United States to evaluate the equipment, staff, and other resources involved in using TIGER files. This project lasted for one year. The conclusion was not positive—"the TIGER Test indicated that none of the products were designed to do what the librarians needed, which was to work from raw TIGER files" (Lang, 1992, p. 880). Major reasons of the failure included insufficient hardware and insufficient time for training.

Right after the TIGER Test ended, the Association of Research Libraries GIS Literacy Project started in the spring of 1992. This project's goal included educating librarians on the GIS skills, improving public access to electronic spatial data like TIGER files, and promoting GIS technology to users. This project started with 31 research libraries in 1992. The number of participating libraries increased to 64 in 1993 (Kollen and Baldwin, 1993). The Environment System Research Institute donated ArcView and ready-to-use data (ArcUSA and ArcWorld) to this project. Unlike TIGER Test, this project was successful. It helped the libraries to start GIS services. Terry

Strasser, senior librarian at the New York State Library, found that this project gave them the impetus they needed. She doubts that the state library would have developed data and mapping services as extensively without this project (Yu, 1996).

Project Alexandria was funded by the National Science Foundation (NSF), the National Aeronautics and Space Administration (NASA) and the Advanced Research Projects Agency (ARPA). Six libraries participated the project to study the online access to spatial data. Beard (Beard, 1995)described the Alexandria project in University of California at Santa Barbara. The project started in October 1994 and is expected to run to late 1997. This project aims to develop a distributed digital library that provides access to geographic referenced information, including maps, remote-sensing images, and pictorial and textual information. Internet will be used to connect the participating libraries.

In addition to these large scale projects, many libraries have begun to provide GIS services to their patrons, including some public libraries. St. Louis Public Library started to provide GIS services as early as 1992 (Watts, 1993). The library provided public access to GIS to all the library patrons. Typical patrons are from the not-for-profit community and students working in the health care field. Others are small business developers working on business plans.

GIS USER SERVICES IN LIBRARIES

Because of their different resources in personnel, hardware, software, and data, libraries are providing different kinds and levels of services to their patrons. This section will list the types of services identified through a review of the literature.

TIGER File Check Out and FTP Service

The University of Arizona allowed users to check out TIGER CD-ROMs in 1993, partly because the library was not equipped with GIS at that time (Kollen and Baldwin, 1993). The SUNY at Albany library also provides this service. Users who check out TIGER files are usually experienced GIS users. They have computers and GIS software, but don't want to buy TIGER CD-ROMs from the Census Bureau.

Some libraries enable users to get access to the TIGER and other Census files through FTP. Cornell University's Mann Library permits patrons to transfer files to their local workstations. Chiang and Rieger (Chiang and Rieger, 1995) of Mann Library consider this an essential service to users. They point out that GIS files are usually too big to fit on diskettes. Therefore, FTP is an appropriate method. Pilot FTP projects have been run by other libraries. For example, the University of California offered anonymous FTP service to 1994 TIGER files shortly after they were published.

Produce Maps for Patrons

New York State Library is able to create thematic maps at a patron's request. This kind of service requires librarians with extensive GIS knowledge and skills. Libraries also need to have hardware, software, and data to support the service.

Open Access to Patrons

Kollen and Baldwin's survey (Kollen and Baldwin, 1993) in 1993 showed that two-thirds of the participant libraries allowed patrons to use the GIS workstation with no supervision. Some libraries screened GIS users, and one library limited use to 'primary clientele.' Typically, users require librarian assistance. It is possible to take more of the librarian's time in this manner than by simply producing maps for patrons. However, this kind of service has a user education function and promotes GIS usage. Users may also get a more satisfactory map by creating it themselves.

GIS User Education

Lang (Lang, 1992) pointed out that education is essential to make the technology's introduction in libraries a success. GIS has introduced a new way of thinking about maps, similar to the way that computer programming teaches a new method of thinking in solving problems. "Maps in a GIS are like the answers to questions–whereas traditional maps answer a range of questions and have to be interpreted by the user. Researchers need to be shown what GIS can do and what they can ask of it" (Lang, 1992, p. 882).

At the University of Connecticut Library, a number of 'how to' devices have been developed to introduce the user to MapInfo for Windows. The next level of instruction is a mixture of education and training. The library has also organized a series of GIS seminars. Topics ranged from a general overview of GIS to the statistical analysis of spatial data (McGlamery, 1995).

CHALLENGES IN USING GIS IN LIBRARIES

Providing GIS service in libraries is not that easy. Kollen indicated that the installation and application of GIS in research libraries is moving much more slowly than predicted. This section will examine some major factors that may affect the diffusion of GIS in libraries.

Organization

In Lang's article (Lang, 1992), Cox indicated that the challenge for getting the public to use the system is in organization. Libraries need to determine the public demand for data and then find the easiest way to provide access. One question is whether libraries are the appropriate place for dissemination of GIS maps and data. He stated that "GIS is creating new, visible, strong roles for libraries" (Lang, 1992, p 883). He believed that libraries are right places to provide GIS services because, (1) libraries are neutral institutions without bias, and (2) the library system infrastructure is well established; people think of libraries when they need information.

Budget

GIS requires sophisticated hardware and expensive software which may not be in accordance with the libraries' budgets. Should the libraries spend large amounts of money on the access of highly selective data by a small group of clients? A negative answer may not sound unreasonable. However, we need to consider this issue over the long run. Libraries play an important role in the diffusion of new knowledge and technology. If patrons can learn geo-thinking from libraries, it will greatly promote the applications of GIS in the community and generate a large revenue for society. On-line database searching was expensive and used only by a small group of patrons years ago, but it has become an important and popular service in libraries today.

Software and Technique

Lang (Lang, 1992), said that the main challenges are finding software that is easy to use and bringing the products into the mainstream of library operation. It is difficult to make a GIS software that is intuitive. Students at the University of Washington Libraries complained about the system documents and the on-line help. In a survey conducted by Kollen and Baldwin (Kollen and Baldwin, 1993), in 1993, librarians indicated that ArcView is not user friendly. They complained that ArcView's documentation is not satisfactory and that too much time is needed for training. This sounds conflicted with the statement Lang cited (Lang, 1992, p. 882): "We've found, though, if someone works with ArcView for just a couple of hours, they can really use it." It seems that further qualitative and quantitative studies need to be conducted to examine whether ArcView can be easily mastered by new users.

When libraries select GIS software, it is often true that users prefer the low-end products because they have fewer functions and are simple to use. ArcView 2.0 is a great package with object-oriented programming language support, but it may make newcomers confused because of its numerous command buttons and menu options. In this case, librarians should make certain changes to the user interface to make them easy to understand and easy to use.

Librarians' GIS Literacy

Lang indicated that there is a wide range of computer and GIS expertise among librarians. Some librarians are experienced GIS experts, while others have much to learn about hardware, GIS software, and GIS theories. Most of the librarians have strong backgrounds in library science. Some have backgrounds in computer science. Computer literacy is critical in learning GIS. In addition, librarians need to study the GIS basic theories systematically, including topology (point, line, and polygon), cartography, and map overlay concepts. During an interview (Yu, 1996), one librarian complained about not having enough time to work on GIS although she was assigned to coordinate the GIS service in her library. In this case, the library director should redefine a new job position and ensure the training for the librarian. The interview also suggested that it might be easier for a librarian with computer background to learn GIS than a librarian with background in geography.

Users' GIS Literacy

Hiller and Johnson described the GIS at the University of Washington Libraries. The University Library provided GIS services as early as 1989. Students in the school of Geography used the system to do their assignments. Students experienced difficulties with GIS. Understanding census data was not easy for them, and mapping systems were also difficult. Each undergraduate user required more than 30 minutes of one-on-one introductory demonstration and explanation, which still could not guarantee success in map making. They had problems in data selection and data classification (Hiller and Johnson, 1989).

User education is necessary to improve GIS literacy. As the University of Connecticut Library demonstrated, seminars and on-line training programs are all efficient and effective methods of providing user education.

Collaboration with Other Departments

Kollen and Baldwin (Kollen and Baldwin, 1993) stated that map libraries are increasingly collaborating with faculty in other departments on the university campuses, government agencies, and related private companies. For example, the staff at the University of Arizona Map Collection have developed various liaison opportunities throughout the university. In Kollen's 1993 survey, 70% of the members of one user group have close relationships to the departments of Geography, Urban Planning, Demography, Social Science, Political Science, and Environmental Science.

GIS Usage Level

It has been noticed that most GIS services in libraries are used at the lowest level—making maps. As described in the second section, the major advantage of GIS is its organizational and analytical capability. There are two issues involved here. One is users' knowledge of GIS. If they see GIS as a map maker only, they will not make higher demands on GIS service in libraries. The next issue becomes a policy issue. If users have more sophisticated GIS demands, should the library provide the enhanced service? If the answer is yes, what if the patron is a private company? Should libraries help the private sector to make more profit using services provided through taxpayers' money? What is the appropriate level of service that libraries should provide? These questions need to be explored. There may be a long debate and it may never be fully resolved.

Objectives of GIS Services in Libraries

As described in the previous sections, the objectives of both the TIGER Test and ARL's project involve promoting the use of TIGER files. It seems that one of the reasons libraries should provide GIS service is to let those CD-ROMs out of their cages. However, the fact is that TIGER cannot be used directly. In Kollen and Baldwin's survey, only two of 23 respondents have produced maps from TIGER files and Census data using ArcView because ArcView 1.0 didn't have the function needed to convert TIGER files into map coverages.

It is more practical for libraries to purchase map data from third parties, such as Wessex. These third parties' data are more or less from TIGER files, but have been processed so that they can be used directly by GIS software. Libraries can produce the same data using TIGER and GIS software, but it is time consuming and probably not cost efficient either.

The objective of GIS services in libraries may be better understood as providing a new research tool with which to use the data in libraries. TIGER Test and ARL's GIS project did not really let users use TIGER directly, but they did generate libraries interest in GIS and promote GIS as part of the reference services.

Treatment of GIS Generated Maps

Kollen and Baldwin raised a question: "What do we do with the new maps created by GIS? Do we retain them or give them away? Do we provide cataloging for future access?" (Kollen and Baldwin, 1993, p. 26).

The result of their survey shows that almost all the participants are willing to give the map to the user, and half will keep either a print copy or save the electronic file. One respondent has cataloged the print copies.

The survey result showed that half of the librarians in 1993 did not really understand the difference between paper maps and GIS. They treated GIS as simply a map maker and didn't get the idea that GIS should be used to create new information to fill users' needs. Regardless of how much space the copies take (either physical space for hard copies or disk space for electronic files), it is more difficult for users to retrieve the maps that fit their needs exactly (if there are any) than to make a new map using the available variables. Having all the user-generated maps cataloged is more expensive and does not help either. Making maps is an art. Ten people with the same interest may create ten different maps. Selecting the scale and determining the data range are all based on personal preference or bias.

This is not to say that libraries should provide only raw data and software requiring patrons start from scratch each time they need a map. Libraries may create some of the most-frequently used base maps in an electronic version. Users can use those maps directly and make changes as they wish. This approach is different from saving all the user-generated maps. The former aims at providing a higher starting point for the users' creative work; the latter is intended to let the users use maps generated by others.

USER ACCESS TO GIS

According to the literature, GIS users mainly are researchers, university faculty members, students, not-for-profit community workers, and small business developers working on business plans. All the articles point out that GIS software is still hard for users to use. For example:

- St. Louis Public Library (Watts, 1993),–Many patrons have required staff assistance working with the system. Some are able to proceed independently using a one-page sheet of very basic instructions.

- University of Washington Libraries–"Beyond the complexity of the great amount of data available to the system user, the mapping system is also difficult for unsophisticated users to follow, even with its menu aspects" (Hiller and Johnson, 1989, p. 89). It is reported that each undergraduate user required more than thirty minutes of one-on-one assistance.

- The result of Kollen and Baldwin's (Kollen and Baldwin, 1993), survey shows that "almost overwhelmingly, respondents believe that users will need a lot of assistance to produce maps, ranging up to four hours."

The high demand on librarians' time may be too much for libraries to handle. On the other hand, the sharp learning curve of GIS may stop many users from trying without some guidance. What should libraries do? Should we wait until GIS software is user-friendly enough for patrons to use intuitively?

Zwart (Zwart, 1993) studied the diffusion of GIS technology. He points out that there is evidence to suggest that users may be satisfied with relatively simple tools to undertake comparatively well-defined tasks on straightforward and simple systems. His study shows that users tend to use fewer commands than what the system provides. The commands are different depending on the user group. In other words, the simpler the system is, the better users like it. The controversy exists because GIS software producers tend to create powerful GIS packages. Although the user interface is becoming more and more friendly, more and more functions are being offered. Given this situation, libraries can play an important role as intermediaries between users and GIS software.

Online database searching was the librarian's job several years ago. Users at that time saw that as one of the librarian's special techniques. Today, many clients can search bibliographic databases on CD-ROM themselves. It should be noted that many of these database searchers still do not know how to perform sophisticated searches, such as specifying whether two terms have to be together or not more than three terms apart. The CD-ROM user interface simplifies the online system and some features, but has been accepted by most of the users. Some systems have different modes for people with different backgrounds in information retrieval, e.g., Browse and Expert modes in the Wilson system.

Libraries can do the same to promote GIS to users. Here are some suggestions to improve user access to library GIS services:

1. *Simplified User Interfaces.* It is hard to expect GIS producers to provide over-simplified products specifically for certain user groups. However, new GIS software, such as ArcView 2.0 from ESRI, supports

programming language which can be used to customize the user interface. Librarians know their clients' interests and their GIS and computer literacy levels. The library should not be merely a free computer lab, it should be an active, value-add agency and encourage people to use GIS. It is the library's duty to create user interfaces that meet the tastes of their specific user group. Libraries should not only make the user interface intuitive and friendly, they should also make it simple for certain users. If a group of users need only eight command buttons, having 20 command buttons showing on screen simply makes them confused.

2. *Multiple Levels of Usage.* As stated at the beginning of this paper, GIS is not simply a map maker. It is a powerful tool to perform analysis. The simplified user interface may make a big group of people happy, but not those who have a GIS background or know more about computers. For example, data prepared by libraries may be enough for naive GIS users to generate a satisfactory result. Experienced users, however, may want to put their own data in the system to perform analysis. The latter demands more GIS functions to transform text information into map locations. Similar to the different modes offered in document retrieval systems, libraries may create several GIS user interfaces with different level of complexity.

3. *Easy to Understand Data.* Data should be available in an easy to understand format. Librarians may not be able to expect patrons to have knowledge of GIS, even in relational databases. Hiller and Johnson summarized the three key steps to use GIS: "Most users have not readily grasped the three-step sequence: (1) establishing two separate data sets, one geographic and the other thematic, through completely separate processes; (2) merging of these data sets to give geographic meaning to the thematic information; and (3) manipulating the graphics to provide a truly meaningful map" (Hiller and Johnson, 1989, p. 89). A large percentage of patrons may only be able to handle the third step–playing with the system to generate a favorite map. The first two steps are not easy at all. A librarian made a study on how fast librarians can learn to extract census data (Zwart, 1993). The result showed that no one did that within two hours. It can be imagined how hard that task is for an ordinary patron. If the first two steps that Hiller and Johnson indicated can be automated, users will feel more comfortable using GIS.

Geographic Coverage

A digital base map which has the topology established and can be processed by a GIS is called a coverage. Other attribute data can be linked to the coverage to generate various maps. Unless users need to include their own geographic data (such as a list of addresses to geocode) in the analysis, libraries should provide users with ready-to-use base maps. It is impractical to let a user develop a geographic coverage using TIGER in a library–it takes a long time and it requires special procedures far beyond an ordinary user's knowledge. This has been proved by previous pilot GIS projects in libraries. Libraries should have some frequently used geographic coverages prepared and stored on a server. For example, a library in New York City may have geographic coverages of New York City and New York State, while a library in Los Angles may store those of Los Angeles and California. Street, highway system, water system, county boundaries, census tract boundaries, and zip code boundaries are all frequently demanded coverages.

Attribute Data

Geographic coverages themselves do not mean much to users. Users need attribute data to perform analysis and to generate maps and tables. This requires a step to link the attributes to the geographic features. In a relational database system, a 'key' needs to be designated in both databases. The system can then compare the value of the keys to bring the data from attribute database to the GIS database.

This process can be automated and run quietly in the background. In other words, users do not have to select the keys in the databases and perform the file-join step by step in the right sequence. The system should simply ask users 'what variables are you interested in.' The system then should be smart enough to know which attribute database it should open and which field should be used as the key. To users, they may not necessarily know what is going on and may consider selecting variables as a simple task.

Libraries should use easy-to-understand text to represent fields. In Census files like STF-3A, field names do not reflect the content of the fields. Users need to look in a data dictionary to understand what A000001 means. This is an annoying job, even for a GIS professional. Libraries can make the user interface in such a way that users pick attributes from the English field description. When a user clicks the mouse on the description text, the computer should find out what the field name is and perform the link in the background.

Figures 4 through 6 illustrate the idea discussed above. Figure 4 is the standard ArcView2 user interface. Users can select View, Table, Charts, and other objects. There is a set of command buttons for each of these objects. The command buttons in Figure 4 are the default command buttons for View. Users need to select a map coverage, select variables to

FIGURE 4. Standard ArcView2 User Interface

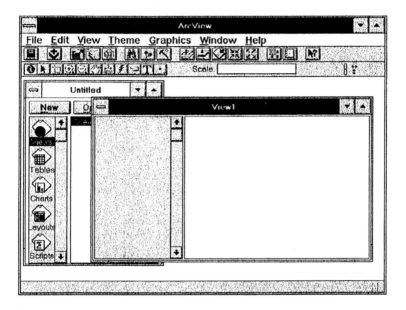

map, join databases if necessary, and design output format to make a thematic map. This is too much for a beginner to learn and use. Figure 5 and Figure 6 illustrate a set of simplified command buttons and a simplified procedure to guide users to go step by step. When a library patron selects the EASY user interface, the patron will see a screen like Figure 5 asking him/her to choose geographic location (state and county), data analysis level (State, County, or Census Tract), and attributes to study. Two text windows explain the population and note about each variable. The Advanced Search function can help users to find the interested attributes by keywords. The Calculate function enables users to obtain data by calculation using attributes in the data file. This function is especially valuable to the Census file users. For example, a patron needs to sum the population at the age of 20, 21, 22 to 24, and 25 to 29 years old to get the number of people who are between 20 and 30 years old. The patron may further need to divide that number by the total population to get the percentage. With a program like Figure 5, all the tasks of data selecting, file joining, and calculating can be done in a "black box."

Figure 6 is a simplified user interface of ArcView2. In Figure 6, only the command buttons are modified to demonstrate the idea of simplified

FIGURE 5. Start Screen for Beginners

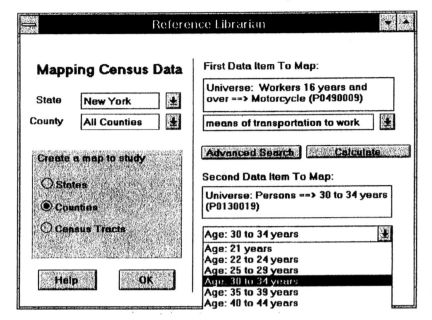

user interface. In practice, menus should be modified to suit the users' needs too. Comparing with Figure 4, many command buttons are removed. The command buttons left enable users to change the map scale, zoom in or zoom out, add text or label, and measure distance between geographic features. It also integrates the print process to one command button. When the printer button is clicked, the computer will print the map using a pre-defined layout.

More research needs to be done to study appropriate user interfaces for different user groups. It can be expected that GIS is more user friendly and easier to use when more and more work is done automatically in the background.

CONCLUSION

Libraries, especially map libraries, are facing a transition from preserving and accessing paper maps to providing digital spatial data services. GIS brings a new way of thinking for libraries and patrons. Technology and data for Geographic Information Systems and an understanding

FIGURE 6. Simplified ArcView User Interface (Data Used In This Map Are Not Real Data)

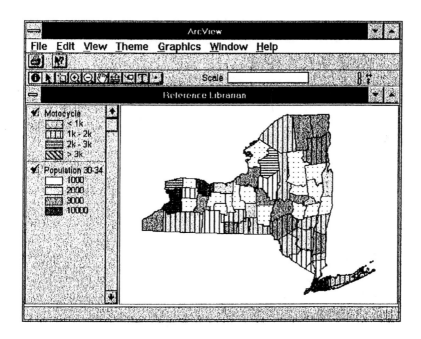

among librarians of the processes and issues have grown steadily. More and more libraries are providing GIS services. Many policy issues, organization issues, and technique issues still need further study and testing to improve the quality of the services. An important issue facing libraries is how to make the GIS accessible and usable by users. Libraries should develop multi-level, intuitive, and user friendly GIS user interfaces to enable users to use GIS without much hassle.

REFERENCES

Beard, K. (1995, June). "Digital spatial libraries: A context for engineering and library collaboration," *Information Technology and Libraries* 14 no. 2, 79-85.

Castle, Gilbert III, ed. *(1993)*. *Profiting from a Geographic Information System.* Fort Collins: GIS World.

Chiang, K. S., Rieger, O. Y. (1995). "Introduction to extracting and mapping census data," *Reference Services Review* (US), 23 no. 1, 29-38.

Dangermond, Jack. (1990). "A classification of software components commonly used in geographic information systems," In Donna J. Peuquet and Duane F. Marble, ed. *Introductory Readings in Geographic Information Systems.* New York: Taylor & Francis.

ESRI. (1991). *Understanding GIS.* Redlands: ESRI.

Hiller, S., Johnson, M. (1989). "Public access computer-assisted mapping and the instructional program," *Reference Services Review* (US) 17, no. 4, 87-90.

Kollen, Christine; Baldwin, Charlene M. (1993, September). "Automation and map librarianship: three issues," *Bulletin (Special Libraries Association. Geography and Map Division)* no. 173, 24-38.

Lai, Ponchin and Gillies, Charles F. (1991). "The impact of geographical information systems on the role of spatial data libraries," *International Journal of GIS,* 5, no. 2, 241-251.

Lang, L. (1992, November). "Mapping the future of map librarianship," *American Libraries* 23 no. 10, 880-885.

Larsgaard, M. L. & L. Carver. (1995, June). "Accessing spatial data online: Project Alexandria," *Information Technology and Libraries* 14 no. 2, p. 93-97.

Marble, Duane F. (1984). "Geographic information systems: an overview," In *Proceedings, Pecora 9 Conference, Sioux Falls, S.D.,* 18-24.

McGlamery, P. (1995, June). "Identifying issues and concerns: the University of Connecticut's MAGIC—a case study," *Information Technology and Libraries* 14, no. 2, 116-121.

Watts, Anne, and Charles P. Kofron. (1993, April). "The St. Louis Public Library's electronic atlas: geographic information systems (GIS) in the public library environment," *Illinois Libraries,* vol. 75, 173-5.

Yu, May. (1996). *Master dissertation: geographic information systems in capital district libraries* (Albany: State University of New York At Albany).

Zwart, Peter R. (1993). "Embodied GIS—A Concept for GIS Diffusion," In Ian Masser and Harlan J. Onsrud, ed. *Diffusion and Use of Geographic Information Technologies,* Boston: Kluwer Academic.

BIBLIOGRAPHY

Adler, Prudence S. & Donna P. Koepp. (1992). "Association of Research Libraries Geographic Information Systems Literacy Project," *Meridian.* no. 7, p. 45-6.

Armento, Greg. (1988, December). "Geographic information systems," *Bulletin (Special Libraries Association. Geography and Map Division)* no. 154, p. 33-5.

Barron, Daniel D. (1995, January). "Bringing the world and information together: geographic information systems for education," *School Library Media Activities Monthly* vol. 11, p. 49-50.

Blair, N. L. & C. J. Manson. (1994). "Need for a national geologic mapping index database," in *Finding and Communicating Geoscience Information, Proceedings of the Twenty-Eighth Meeting of the Geoscience Information Society,*

October 1993, Boston, MA (Bloomington: Geoscience Information Society) p. 179- 195.

Chiang, Katherine S. (1994). "Sidebar 3: geographic information systems; services at Mann Library," *Library Hi Tech* 12 no. 3, p. 53.

Clarke, Keith C. (1985, December). "Geographic information systems: definitions and prospects," *Bulletin (Special Libraries Association. Geography and Map Division)* no. 142, p. 12-17.

Cline, N. M. & Prudence Adler. (1995, June). "GIS and research libraries: one perspective," *Information Technology and Libraries* 14, no. 2, p. 111-115.

Cobb, D. A. (1994). "Layer upon layer: mystery upon mystery," in *Finding and Communicating Geoscience Information, Proceedings of the Twenty-Eighth Meeting of the Geoscience Information Society, October 1993, Boston, MA* (Bloomington: Geoscience Information Society), p. 39-43.

Cooke, Constance B, Michael Prisloe. (1990). "Geographic information systems in Connecticut" in *International Association of Marine Science Libraries and Information Centers. Conference (15th: 1989: St George's, Bermuda). IAMSLIC at a crossroads* (International Assn. of Marine Science Libs. and Information Centers), p. 171-3.

Cox, Allan B. (1995). An Overview to Geographic Information Systems. *Journal of Academic Librarianship 21* no. 4, p. 237-49.

Dalrymple, Helen. (1994, April). "ArcInfo map collection donated to Library," *Library of Congress Information Bulletin* vol. 53, p. 141-2.

Fiegel, F. (1995). "The map library of the bibliotheque interuniversitaire scientifique (Jussieu: future prospects. La cartotheque du Cadist de l'Univerite de Jussieu perspectives d'avenir)," *Bulletin des Bibliotheques de France* 40 no. 3, p. 58-62.

Frank, S. (1994, September-October). "Cataloging digital geographic data in the information infrastructure: a literature and technology review," *Information and Management* 30 no. 5, p. 587-606.

Graziani, M. E. & O. Kays. *(1986). Computer-based library reference system* (Washington: USGS).

Jones, Alan D. (1993, November). "Where do all the good books go? Geographic information systems and the local library–Mapping the geographic distribution of users of Armidale Public Library," *Australian Library Journal* vol. 42, p. 241-9.

"Key terms–relating to geographic information systems," *(1995, June). Information Technology and Libraries.* vol. 14, p. 122.

LaGuardia, Cheryl & Michael Blake. (1995, June 1). "CD-ROM review. (geographic software evaluation)," *Library Journal* 12, no. 10, p. 176(4).

Lutz, M. (1995, June). "Making GIS a part of library service," *Information Technology and Libraries* 14 no. 2, p. 77-78.

Mangan, E. U. (1995, June). "The making of a standard," *Information Technology and Libraries* 14 no. 2, p. 99-110.

McGlamery, Patrick & Melissa Lamont. (1994, December). "New opportunities and challenges: geographic information systems in libraries," *Database* 17 no. 6, p. 35-44.

Moritz, Tom. (1990). "Geographic information systems: a selective review and introduction," in *International Association of Marine Science Libraries and Information Centers. Conference (15th: 1989: St George's, Bermuda). IAM-SLIC at a crossroads* (International Assn. of Marine Science Libs. and Information Centers) p. 167-9.

Nag, P. (1993). "Role of geographical information system and communication technology in thematic mapping," in *Advances in Library and Information Science* Vol. 4: *Informal Communication* (Jodhpur, Scientific Publishers) p. 103-118.

Oppenheim, C. (1994). "LISLEX–legal issues of concern to the library and information sector," *Journal of Information Science* 20, no. 4, p. 285-287.

Rand, R. Y. (1995, June). "Assisted Search for Knowledge (ASK): a navigational tool set to global change data and information," *Information Technology and Libraries* 14 no. 2, p. 87-91.

Scott, R. L. (1994). "Geoscience resources on the Internet," *Reference Librarian* no. 41-42, p. 55-64.

Smith, Phyllis. (1993, June). "GIS–is it contagious?" *Arkansas Libraries* vol. 50, p. 10.

Troselius, Renee. (1994, May). "The Software Toolworks World Atlas," *Wilson Library Bulletin* 68 no. 9, p 115(2).

"Wilson Foundation supports GIS." *(1993, January). Wilson Library Bulletin* vol. 67, p. 14.

Wondra, Phil. (1989, March). "Geographic information systems in the National Park Service," *Bulletin (Special Libraries Association. Geography and Map Division)* no. 155, p. 12-15.

MANAGING
ELECTRONIC RESOURCES

Managing Reference Services in the Electronic Age: A Competing Values Approach to Effectiveness

Virginia A. Papandrea

SUMMARY. Managing reference services is challenged by the influx of electronic resources in libraries. Traditional approaches to reference management lack a conceptual framework of effectiveness and emphasize mostly internal processes, downplaying the turbulent environments libraries face. The competing values approach to effectiveness is presented as a broad-based integration of four existing models of organizational effectiveness, encompassing the contradic-

Virginia A. Papandrea is Assistant to the Dean, School of Information Science and Policy, and a doctoral candidate in the Department of Public Administration, University at Albany, State University of New York, 135 Western Avenue, Draper 113, Albany, NY 12222. E-mail: papand@cnsvax.albany.edu

[Haworth co-indexing entry note]: "Managing Reference Services in the Electronic Age: A Competing Values Approach to Effectiveness." Papandrea, Virginia A. Co-published simultaneously in *The Reference Librarian* (The Haworth Press, Inc.) No. 60, 1998, pp. 111-126; and: *Electronic Resources: Use and User Behavior* (ed: Hemalata Iyer) The Haworth Press, Inc., 1998, pp. 111-126. Single or multiple copies of this article are available for a fee from The Haworth Document Delivery Service [1-800-342-9678, 9:00 a.m. - 5:00 p.m. (EST). E-mail address: getinfo@haworth.com].

tory values of an internal and an external focus, a control and a flexibility orientation, and means and ends. Implications of the approach for reference management are discussed, and the movement toward diversified team structures examined as a possible solution to the problems of managing reference in the electronic age. The focus is on academic libraries but may apply to other types of libraries as well. *[Article copies available for a fee from The Haworth Document Delivery Service: 1-800-342-9678. E-mail address: getinfo@haworth.com]*

INTRODUCTION

In the latest edition of his textbook on reference work, Bill Katz offers a succinct definition of the job of the reference librarian: "Reference librarians answer questions."[1] This definition is, however, deceptively simple. The increasing complexity of the reference librarian's role can be inferred from Katz's summary of the major ongoing developments in reference services:

- The shift in importance from the reference desk to the electronic data center;
- Reference librarians' continued and increasing subject and technical expertise;
- Increasing reliance on computer technologies to assist users;
- Growth in the role among reference librarians of research advisor.[2]

Katz also notes the dominant trends–largely the result of forces in the environment–that now affect reference services:

- The growth of networked information and of the librarian's role to mediate between the mass of disorganized data and the needs of clients;
- Increased availability of databases over networks, and the need for librarians to solve problems clients experience in using them;
- The likelihood that new technologies will increase the number of reference services;
- The need for librarians to continuously upgrade their skills in using the new technologies;
- The increased importance of subject mastery, as sources become more specialized and users become more sophisticated;
- Continued growth in demand for instruction in the use of resources.[3]

The picture of reference services that emerges from these changes and trends is hardly a simple one. The influx of electronic information and technologies such as the Internet, CD-ROM indexes, networked workstations, and full-text databases, changes the what, how, when, and where of "answering questions," and the degree to which librarians feel competent to do so. To those who have been working in or around libraries over the last decade, this statement, and the trends and changes Katz lists, are obvious. To those new to the library profession, or whose libraries have not been heavily inundated with information technologies, they may be less so.

A similar comment could be made about other trends affecting libraries in general and reference work in particular. Fairly obvious to many are demographic shifts that are bringing an increasingly diverse clientele and work force into all work places, including libraries. Diversity includes many dimensions: age, ethnic background, skill level, and specialization of interests. National and global economic forces are resulting in shrinking budgets for many libraries, eroding their ability to expand or maintain staff, collections, and other resources. As Schloman points out, tight budgets also force library decision makers to examine carefully the balance between implementing new technologies and continuing to offer traditional services.[4] Libraries are expected to continue to make print resources and traditional services available while grafting new resources and services onto existing ones. Libraries are also being pressured by clients to make more information available more quickly and conveniently, at little or no cost to themselves, from all over the globe.

Adding to the stress of coping with environmental changes, many libraries are responding by experimenting with new organizational arrangements which are themselves stressful, including closer relationships with academic computing organizations. Given the pressures and demands on reference librarians, it is little wonder that there is widespread complaint of burnout in the profession.

This paper examines the implications for reference management of the changes outlined above, most particularly changes attending the implementation of information technologies in reference services. A framework for effective management is presented, and the challenges of managing the reference function cast within prevailing theories of organizational effectiveness. The movement toward team structures is examined as a possible answer to the problems of managing in a turbulent environment. The discussion focuses on academic libraries, but may apply as well to other types of libraries.

THE STATE OF REFERENCE MANAGEMENT

Pressures on reference services are being felt keenly by those charged with managing them. In most libraries this responsibility continues to be that of a head of reference, although in recent years librarians have experimented with different structural arrangements such as teams or leadership rotation. Even where there is a head of reference, management tasks (e.g., coordination of networked services or of user education) may be distributed among department members.[5] King commented nearly a decade ago on the reluctance of reference librarians to take on the manager's role, citing librarians' preference, on the one hand, for doing reference work, and on the other, for avoiding the headaches and pressures of administration.[6] Distributing the managerial workload across the reference department provides some relief to the head of reference. It also gives reference staff opportunities to develop managerial skills without necessarily transferring such managerial responsibilities as overall coordination, performance evaluation, budgetary oversight, or liaison with top management.

Reflections from librarians on the role and responsibilities of reference management have traditionally tended to emphasize internal processes such as communicating, facilitating group cohesion, planning services, coaching and evaluating staff performance, and codifying internal policies into a manual. As recently as 1982, virtually all of the essays in Katz and Fraley's collection of papers on reference management were internally focused. Fraley, in her preface to this work, expresses the then prevailing orientation toward management:

> Management is the act of motivating individuals to make work decisions that meet personal, departmental, and organizational goals so that all are congruent. When managers actually describe their routine activities, most, directly or indirectly, are concerned with personnel.[7]

Times have changed. The influx into reference work of information technologies and the problems that accompany these technologies have broadened the range of concerns expressed by those who manage reference services. There is still, of course, attention to internal matters such as personnel issues and communication. But there are many additional matters demanding that managerial attention be focused outside the reference department. Reference management increasingly encompasses relationships with the external environment, including demands from an increasingly diverse clientele, changing technologies, the economy, and the legal and policy issues of information.

The internal focus has expanded as well, to include deep concerns about the need to continuously upgrade reference librarians' technical skills to deal with new technologies; issues of burnout and technostress; and the ability of reference managers to influence decision making concerning the acquisition of needed–often expensive–resources. The time frame for decision making has also changed, with more long-range and strategic planning being incorporated into managerial roles.

Reference managers are also looking critically at the design of their organizations. New structural arrangements—in use or prescribed—being reported in the professional literature are largely in response to changes in technology and related pressures from the environment. Librarians, like inhabitants of other organizations facing similar pressures, are viewing flattened hierarchies, teams, and matrix organizations as more able than traditional hierarchies to respond quickly to changes and opportunities in the environment, and to the needs of clients or customers.[8] Some of these experiments and prescriptions apply to the reference department per se, while others are intended for the library as a whole.[9] Still others involve closer ties or even mergers between user services staff in computing centers and library reference units. While some of these reorganizations are intended to increase efficiency and effectiveness, other arguments for restructuring are based on a desire to redistribute decision-making responsibility from the exclusive purview of top or middle management to organizational members at large, thereby lessening the distance between the highest and lowest rungs of the organizational hierarchy.

Tacit assumptions about effectiveness appear to underlie arguments for a particular structure and its attendant processes, e.g., assumptions that flatter organizations will meet user needs more effectively than will a bureaucratic organization.[10] Notably absent from most of the current discussion on reference management, however, is an overall conceptual framework of organizational effectiveness for analysis or practice. Although words like "effective" or "successful" permeate discussions of the evaluation of reference service or individual performance, little or no attention is given to a definition of effectiveness itself, to the dimensions that comprise it, or to the criteria by which it is to be measured.

Such abstractions as effectiveness receive considerable attention, however, in the field of organization studies. In fact library professional literature on managerial topics is liberally sprinkled with references to the work of researchers in organization theory and behavior, as well as works by those who have popularized such research for management practitioners. This is an indication that the field of organization studies has much to offer the library profession as it grapples with the challenges of "organizing" to perform its vital mission of serving the changing information needs of client groups in a turbulent environment. It is appropriate, then, to turn to a framework of effectiveness developed by organization researchers to enrich the discussion of how best to meet the challenges of managing reference services today.

A FRAMEWORK OF ORGANIZATIONAL EFFECTIVENESS

Organizational theorists have found the definition of effectiveness to be an elusive one. Organizations are collections of complex phenomena existing in dynamic relationships to one another and to a continually shifting, multi-faceted environment. What is effective for one aspect of the organization (e.g., maintaining a stable work climate in which professionals feel competent to perform their jobs) may not be effective for another (e.g., implementing new technologies to meet increased demands for services). Thus managers are perennially torn between competing demands and conflicting values (such as the need for stability vis à vis the desire for innovation), in an effort to pursue that elusive ideal of effectiveness.

The amorphous nature of organizational effectiveness has generated numerous theories and models regarding how to achieve it. Some of these theories emphasize the performance of individuals, while others address the performance or "survival" of the organization as a whole, or some sub-division thereof. In an effort to make sense of the diffuse theoretical literature on effectiveness, Quinn and Rohrbaugh[11] collected and analyzed criteria of effectiveness used by organizational researchers to evaluate the performance of organizations. From this analysis they derived a four-model integration or framework, primarily comprising existing models of organization. Quinn and Rohrbaugh's framework is called the competing values approach to organizational effectiveness because it encompasses the competing or mutually contradictory sets of values embedded in the models that comprise it.

The competing values framework attempts to locate the various meanings of effectiveness and to portray their relationship to one another. Beyond the theoretical value of the approach, however, lies a practical one. The competing values approach offers the manager a map for thinking about the various competing demands she must meet, and roles she must play, in order to be effective. The competing values approach has several virtues: it encompasses the necessary contradictions or paradoxes of organizational life, such as the need to attend to both internal and external demands; it includes both the structures and controls necessary to support rational decision making and coordination of complex activities, and the need to be flexible and responsive to the ever-changing environment and to organizational members; and it recognizes the necessary tensions between ends or final outcomes, and the means to achieve them.

The competing values framework has appeared at least once in the library literature, in an article by Faerman published in 1993.[12] Faerman's presentation of the framework was couched as a mapping of the territory of management that library managers might follow to deal with change effectively, with special emphasis on the transition to user-centered libraries. Rather than duplicate Faerman's efforts, which are quite detailed, the present discussion will capture the highlights of the framework, particularly as they apply to the ways in which reference managers must deal with the influx of information technologies into reference services.

THE COMPETING VALUES FRAMEWORK

The competing values framework integrates four models of organizational analysis, each encompassing values that are important for effectiveness but that stand in some contradictory or paradoxical relationship to one another. The models differ on three major dimensions, or, put another way, there are three sets of competing value dimensions or "tensions" expressed in the overall framework:

1. Organizational focus–from an internal focus on the performance or well-being of people in the organization, to an external focus on the well-being or survival of the organization itself;
2. Organizational structure–from an emphasis on maintaining stability or control, to an emphasis on flexibility or responsiveness;
3. Organizational means and ends–from an emphasis on organizational processes to an emphasis on final outcomes or ends.

The four models comprising the competing values framework are described below, using activities of the reference department as illustrations. The framework is presented graphically in Figure 1.

The Human Relations Model

This model has an *internal focus* on the well-being of the people in the organization, e.g., reference staff. The *ideal structure* for this model is a flexible one that permits participation and accommodates individual needs and talents, such as teams for various functions or projects (e.g., collection development, electronic services, user education, etc.). The *ends* served in this model are the development and well-being of the organization's human resources. In a reference department, these ends would include the professional development and technical training of reference staff mem-

FIGURE 1. Competing Values Framework

HUMAN RELATIONS MODEL	OPEN SYSTEM MODEL
	Flexibility
Means:	Means:
Cohesion; morale	Flexibility; readiness
Ends:	Ends:
Human resource development	Growth; resources acquisition
Mentor Role	Innovator Role
Group Facilitator Role	Broker Role
Internal Focus	*External Focus*
INTERNAL PROCESS MODEL	**RATIONAL GOAL MODEL**
Means:	Means:
Information management; communication	Planning; goal setting
Ends:	Ends:
Stability; control	Productivity; efficiency
Monitor Role	Producer Role
Coordinator Role	Director Role
	Control

bers, such as course work in programming, or training in various Internet search engines. The creation of positive working conditions and reward systems is another end served in this model. The *means* by which such ends are reached include cohesion-building activities and attention to issues of morale. The job of the manager adhering to this model is to show concern for individuals and to support staff development, cohesion, and morale. The good manager, therefore, must develop the roles of mentor and facilitator to be effective. Implicit in this model is the assumption that high degrees of job satisfaction are associated with positive outcomes for the organization as a whole, but the major focus is on the human aspects of organizational life.

The Internal Process Model

Like the human relations model, the internal process model has an *internal focus*. Rather than emphasizing flexible, responsive structures such as teams, however, this model employs *control structures*. Typically these structures are centralized, with clear lines of authority, such as those from library director to head of public services to head of reference to reference staff. The *ends* to be achieved are stability, control, and the coordination of work. In a reference context, these would be manifested as the provision of consistent, accurate information services through the manager's deployment of staff and resources. The manager in this model would address the issue of finding an agreeable balance between traditional print-based services and electronically mediated ones. The *means* for achieving stability, control, and coordination are information management systems and channels of communication. In a reference department these include smooth scheduling of the information desk and user education activities; record keeping on use of services; creation and codification of service policies and practices into a manual; issuing memos and other communications to update staff on new developments; collection development and maintenance; ongoing evaluation of collections and services, and so on. In today's libraries, internal processes might be enhanced by such innovations as electronic record-keeping and e-mail management systems. The job of the reference manager in this model is to integrate activities and ensure that they run smoothly and adhere to policies. The effective manager in this model must develop roles as a monitor of work-flows and a coordinator of activities. An assumption of this model is that most organizational work is routine and can be fit into ongoing policies and procedures.

The Open System Model

The open system model, as its names suggests, has an *external focus* on the environment, and is concerned with the survival or well-being of the organization or work unit as a whole in dealing with that environment. For the reference department, the environment includes other library departments, the library administration, client groups, campus administration, the computing center, producers and vendors of resources, the labor market for reference librarians, the profession as a whole, the scholarly community at large, the legal environment of information, and information technology itself. Effective performance (or even survival) requires *flexible structures*. These may be either standing work groups, or ad hoc structures such as task groups, liaison activities, or informal meetings, to adapt to the environment or to seek resources and support from it.

In the open system model, the organization (e.g., the reference department) aims at the *ends* of growth (in size, services, influence) and the acquisition of resources (e.g., funds, client support, software, equipment, space). The *means* by which these ends are achieved are flexibility in adapting to the environment (such as responsiveness in meeting the growing demand for Internet services) and readiness to recognize and take advantage of opportunities (such as vendor-sponsored trials of full-text databases). In the innovator role, the job of the reference manager in this model is to generate new ideas and activities; in the broker role, her job is to negotiate for the resources required to carry them out. This model assumes that the organization's boundaries are permeable; that the organization is continuously shaped and reshaped by environmental forces; and that the organization can, in turn, influence its environment.

The Rational Goal Model

This model, like the open system model, has an external focus. Its main concern is the achievement of the organizational mission or goals, which in the case of reference (and academic libraries generally) is to support the research and educational mission of the larger institution. The ideal structure in this model is the traditional bureaucracy, characterized by vertical hierarchy of authority; functional specialization; career longevity to support functional expertise; and policies and procedures to ensure consistent treatment of all clients. Libraries have traditionally been organized as formal bureaucracies, but academic libraries usually have a parallel set of committee or project structures to manage short-term activities that do not fall neatly into one area of specialization. Reference departments, as was mentioned earlier, often distribute managerial tasks across staff to ease the unit head's burden or to foster staff development and cohesion. In this model, the end is productivity and efficiency of operations, i.e., maximizing outputs, and achieving maximum outputs at minimum cost. For example, a reference department might use a combination of professional, paraprofessional, and student staff to maximize the range and depth of electronic services, at the lowest possible cost in salaries and training required. The means for achieving efficiency and productivity are planning and goal-setting processes. The job of the reference manager using this model is to plan service goals, objectives, and priorities, and to set up efficient operations and staffing to meet them. The roles the manager needs to develop for effective performance in this model are producer (ensuring productivity in the achievement of outcomes) and director (directing others to meet organizational goals).

The rational goal model is conceptually linked to the internal process model in that both tend to employ bureaucratic structures and processes to achieve control. Both also tend to value control and efficiency over flexibility toward both human needs and environmental demands. The assumption in both models is that the routine is the normal state of affairs, and that virtually all organizational activity can be encompassed by comprehensive policies and procedures. The rational goal model is, however, more externally focused on issues of maintaining standing and legitimacy within a larger social or institutional context. An important assumption of this model is that the individual's behavior is shaped primarily by one's job role and position in the formal hierarchy; the model pays little or no attention to issues like morale, interpersonal conflict, and the "informal organization" that coexists with the formal structure. It also pays little heed to professional workers' preferences for autonomy and for distributed power in decision making.

Summary and Graphic Presentation of the Competing Values Framework

In summary, the competing values approach incorporates and integrates four models of organizational effectiveness for theory and practice. Any one of these models taken alone is theoretically inadequate to explain everything there is to be known about organizations. As guidelines for action, each model alone is also insufficient to ensure effectiveness in practice. Both for theory and practice, an integration of all four models is necessary. The competing values approach suggests that managers who wish to maximize organizational effectiveness would have to consciously attend to both internal and external issues; set up structures that serve both control and flexibility; and oversee both the ends to be achieved in the long term and the day-by-day processes for achieving them. These concerns have been addressed here at the work unit level, in this case the reference unit of an academic library. The inference to be drawn from this is that a reference department that does not maintain some balance between internal and external matters, between control and flexibility, and between means and ends, proceeds at its own peril.

A graphic presentation[13] (see Figure 1) of the competing values approach summarizes the major characteristics of each model and suggests the tensions or paradoxes inherent in attempting to enact all of them simultaneously.

DISCUSSION

The competing values framework can be employed as a set of guidelines for managerial or leadership skill development. Using the framework as a diagnostic tool, the manager can assess her own abilities to carry out all of the roles suggested, and then seek training and development in the areas in which she is weak. For example, a head of reference might find that she is very effective in the roles of the human relations model (mentor, group facilitator) and the open system model (innovator, broker), but less so in internal process and rational goal roles calling for a stronger orientation toward control and bureaucratic processes. To increase her strengths in the "control" aspects of effectiveness, she might, through courses, workshops, or reading, develop more skill in structuring work, delegating responsibility, strategic planning, setting up record keeping and other information systems, and so on.

There is, however, a weakness in this strategy. As Faerman points out,[14] there may be limits on the ability of any one person to fully master all eight roles when in fact there are inherent paradoxes embedded within them. On an individual level, people vary in their abilities to carry out all of the roles equally well–or in their inclination to embrace all of them to the same degree, even if they become aware of the need for effectiveness in all areas and seek training in those in which they are weak. This variation among individual abilities is especially pronounced where the tension is greatest between the models, that is, where there is the least sharing of values between any two models. In the competing values framework, the least sharing of values occurs between the models that are located in *diagonal opposition* to one another. In contrast, models that are *adjacent* to one another share either an internal or external focus, or a similar bent toward control or flexibility.

The internal process model, for example, is diagonally opposed to the open system model, suggesting that individuals who are proficient in the coordinator and monitor roles of the former might be less likely to have developed skills in the innovator and broker roles of the open system model, and vice versa. A highly innovative librarian who is skilled at getting support to implement new Internet services might see the need to maintain accurate records on their use, or to enhance programming of search engines, but might not have a strong inclination or the skills needed to handle all the necessary information management tasks herself.

A similar analysis could be made for the mentor and facilitator roles of the human relations model, and the producer and director roles of the rational goal model, as these two models are also diagonally opposed to one another. The manager who is extremely goal-oriented and directive, e.g., in making sure that staff meet training deadlines, may be less skilled at getting group members to work well together, or coaching staff through episodes of burnout.

Individual limitations on achieving proficiency in all aspects of effectiveness is one reason organizations exist to begin with. The coordinated efforts of people with specialized skills working in groups are what makes group efforts superior to the efforts of individuals working in isolation on complex tasks. To take this rather obvious point one step further, why not allow group members to share not only in producing their assigned outcomes, but in the management of the production itself? The trend toward participative management and self-managing work groups has been prevalent in organizations for decades. In many reference units, for example, the managerial tasks associated with specialized functions such as user education or electronic services are already distributed among staff members. Such models of distributed management are common in organizations or work units in which much of the work is carried out by professional staff who enter the organization with an overarching set of values and role expectations, including the expectation that professional work be carried out with a high degree of autonomy and participation in decision making.

What is being proposed here is that the reference unit not only share management roles among reference staff members, but that a conscious effort be made to include all aspects of effective management at the frontline level of reference. For some libraries' reference units, this would broaden considerably the definition of management, to include more attention to some control functions, as outlined in the hypothetical case above. The broadening of reference management might also apply particularly to a boundary-spanning role more typically assumed at the upper rungs of the hierarchy. Louis and Yan[15] have argued that the implementation of teams and the increased use of information technologies have pushed boundary activities down the organizational level to the work unit. This migration of boundary work is a natural outcome of the dismantling of bureaucratic structures. Boundary activities include the "open system" activities of seeking support and resources; acting as a spokesperson for the unit with outside actors; and "buffering" activities such as protecting the unit from unreasonable demands.

IMPLICATIONS FOR REFERENCE MANAGEMENT

A broad-based model of effectiveness has a number of implications for the way in which reference management occurs. These implications will be presented here in the form of propositions, in the hope that the less conventional of them will spark discussion and even disagreement about how best to manage reference services in the electronic age.

Proposition 1: Share the burden, share the power, share the fun. Some reference departments are distributing managerial responsibility by rotating the management function across all staff members who are eligible. There are weaknesses in the rotational model, however, the chief of which is that it does not overcome the limitations of individual weaknesses (do you really want the least managerially inclined member of your staff to be the head of reference for a year or two?), or fully take advantage of individual strengths.[16] A preferred model is for individual reference unit members to specialize long-term in managing that function in which they have the most expertise, skill, and leadership potential, and for staff members to cross-train or serve on multiple teams only as appropriate.

Proposition 2: Avoid cloning. Diversify. When hiring or staffing the reference unit, seek a range of skills and perspectives. Look for people who like to do the necessary things reference librarians usually dread, even if it means they may not be as effective as the "typical" reference librarian at the functions reference librarians usually like. The dreaded tasks might include the information management, record keeping, hardware trouble-shooting, and other "control" tasks that are less focused on direct service to users. Why should all reference librarians look alike or have the same job profile? The library's internal labor market may force some of this diversification to occur. As automation shifts work away from technical services, there may be catalogers in need of reassignment whose strengths would make an extremely positive contribution to the reference department. Some needed tasks to which they bring great expertise include indexing and other enhancements to searching tools, and collection development. Background in cataloging might also be of great benefit in online searching and research consultant roles, since catalogers are skilled in subject analysis and often have a broad overview of collection strengths.

Proposition 3: Become entrepreneurs. Rather than depend on upper administration to seek funds and other support, reference librarians with a talent for the brokering and innovating roles should look for sources of support from the environment, and should sell their services to potential markets. This means forming strategic alliances, marketing their services, and being active in the larger institution. Most of all it involves being willing to take risks, including the risk of disapproval or failure.

SUMMARY AND CONCLUSION

The influx of rapidly changing information technologies into reference work, along with other environmental pressures such as demographic and economic shifts, has forced reference managers to rethink structures and processes for carrying out a broad array of new and traditional services. Reference departments have met the need for flexibility and responsiveness by experimenting with non-bureaucratic or neo-bureaucratic structures such as matrix organizations and teams.

The competing values approach is suggested here as a lens for viewing, and a map for guiding, the organization in a time of change by providing a multidimensional approach to organizational effectiveness, conceptualized at the work-group level. In this paper, it is suggested that the dimensions of effectiveness, as outlined in the competing values approach, be operationalized at the group level, such that no one manager or other individual be required to embody all of the roles required for effective management. Instead, the roles and skills of the human relations, internal process, open system, and rational goal models identified by the competing values approach can be distributed among work group or team members, allowing individuals to build on their strengths to contribute to optimum group performance.

REFERENCES

1. Katz, William A. *Introduction to Reference Work*, 7th Ed., Vol. 1. New York: McGraw-Hill, 1997, p. 3.
2. Op. cit., p. 5.
3. Op. cit., p. xvi.
4. Schloman, Barbara F. "Managing Reference Services in an Electronic Environment," *The Reference Librarian* No. 37 (1993): 99-109.
5. Kibbee, Josephine Z. "Organization and Management of Reference and Information Services." In *Reference and Information Services: An Introduction*, edited by Richard E. Boggs and Linda C. Smith. Englewood, CO: Libraries Unlimited, Inc., 1991., pp. 191-206.
6. King, Geraldine. "The Management of Reference Services," *RQ* 26 (1987): 407-9.
7. Fraley, Ruth A. "Successful Management of Reference Services." In *Reference Services Administration and Management*, edited by Bill Katz and Ruth A. Fraley. New York: The Haworth Press, Inc., 1982, p. 2.
8. Schloman, op. cit.; Nofsinger, Mary M., and Bosch, Allan W. "Roles of the Head of Reference: From the 1990s to the 21st Century," *The Reference Librarian*, No. 34 (1994): 87-99; Lewis, David W. "Making Academic Reference Services Work," *College and Research Libraries* 55 (1994): 445-456.

9. Fore, Janet S., Knight, R. Cecelia, and Russell, Carrie. "Leadership for User Services in the Academic Library," *Journal of Library Administration* 19, No. 3/4 (1993): 97-110.

10. Schloman, op. cit.

11. Quinn, Robert E. and Rohrbaugh, John. "A Spatial Model of Effectiveness Criteria: Towards a Competing Values Approach to Organizational Analysis," *Management Science* 29 (1983): 363-377.

12. Faerman, Sue R. "Organizational Change and Leadership Styles," *Journal of Library Administration* 19, No. 3/4 (1993): 55-79. Faerman provides both a useful analysis of the competing values framework and its application to library management, and a thorough review of the literature on the competing values approach.

13. Adapted from Quinn and Rohrbaugh, op. cit., 369.

14. Faerman, op. cit., 64.

15. Louis, Meryl Reis and Yan, Aimin. "The Migration of Organizational Functions to the Work Unit Level: Buffering, Spanning and Bringing Up Boundaries." Working Paper #96-26. Boston: Boston University School of Management, 1996.

16. Perdue, Bob and Piotrowski, Chris. "Supervisory Rotation: Impact on an Academic Library Reference Staff," *RQ* 25 (1986): 361-5.

Patron Attitudes
Toward Computerized and Print Resources:
Discussion and Considerations
for Reference Service

Jane M. Subramanian

SUMMARY. Many patrons in an academic setting have preconceived attitudes regarding the use of particular formats of indexes
and other materials. These attitudes can frequently interfere with a
patron's more successful retrieval of needed resources because of the
use of their preferred format rather than the use of the best means of
access for their information need. The impact of these preconceived
views is explored in terms of providing reference service in the present day. *[Article copies available for a fee from The Haworth Document
Delivery Service: 1-800-342-9678. E-mail address: getinfo@haworth.com]*

With the advent of the information explosion and rapid technological
changes in the present day information world, library patrons find a dramatic transformation in their options for access once inside the library
doors. Everywhere one turns, the media promotes the use of computerized
resources and Internet connections, and as a result, many people in the
country begin to focus solely on the means of access as the overriding
factor, rather than concentrate on the information need itself. Those with
computer expertise frequently view the change in information access with
a much different perspective than those with little or no experience with

---

Jane M. Subramanian is Music Cataloger and Reference Librarian, F.W.
Crumb Memorial Library, SUNY Potsdam, Potsdam, NY 13676.

[Haworth co-indexing entry note]: "Patron Attitudes Toward Computerized and Print Resources:
Discussion and Considerations for Reference Service." Subramanian, Jane M. Co-published simulta-
neously in *The Reference Librarian* (The Haworth Press, Inc.) No. 60, 1998, pp. 127-138; and: *Electron-
ic Resources: Use and User Behavior* (ed: Hemalata Iyer) The Haworth Press, Inc., 1998, pp. 127-138.
Single or multiple copies of this article are available for a fee from The Haworth Document Delivery
Service [1-800-342-9678, 9:00 a.m. - 5:00 p.m. (EST). E-mail address: getinfo@haworth.com].

computers. Both types of library users can present equal difficulties for a reference librarian in an academic setting.

In the days of prevalence of print resources, little choice existed in the method of gaining access to material relevant to a particular subject area. The usual option consisted solely of the choice of one print index over another print source in terms of the specific question and the patron's particular capabilities. The emphasis therefore rested solely on the reference query and the best means to obtain the information needed. With the appearance of computerized resources, the emphasis in the minds of many patrons has shifted from access need to an obsession with the format of the access tool, most often centered on print versus computerized format. This diversion away from focus on the information problem frequently can create an obstacle to successful reference service. Sometimes completely lost in the shuffle is the evaluation of the worth of the material obtained, whatever format is used to obtain either citations or the material itself.

The majority of patrons arrive in the library with a preset notion of the "best" format of tool for information access. In most cases, this pre-formed opinion is based on the patron's own previous experience and what they have found to be the easiest type of material to use. Opinions heard from others and/or written and oral comments seen and heard in the media may also have an impact, particularly if the patron has had little firsthand experience. In addition, faculty comments reflecting their impressions and views can also have significant impact on the preconceived notions of students approaching the academic library.

UNDERLYING ASPECTS

Today's rapid expansion and change in the means of supplying information has left many feeling that they no longer have effective knowledge regarding the path of obtaining information. The information overload problem has been widely recognized and possible solutions have already been discussed in the literature, such as Hopkins' article on the librarian's role in dealing with information overload.[1] With the total volume of available information escalating so precipitously, it becomes difficult even for those very familiar with the newer formats of information access to keep abreast of the location and organization of all of this material. Those with better access to computers have greater opportunity to familiarize themselves with a variety of computer software, as well as simple keyboard commands, while those with little access to computers fall further behind in the process. The widening knowledge gap becomes increasingly evident to the reference librarian as those providing reference service must deal with the extremes of computer competence of patrons arriving in the library.

Rapid periods of change have always had significant impact on human population throughout history, and indeed, libraries have experienced their own share long before this period of transition in information delivery. Although articles such as Freeman's discussion on the earlier impact of library technology[2] and even Socrates' known reluctance to shift from the oral tradition to a written one[3] clearly document similar struggles with change in earlier periods, today's pace of change appears to be far more rapid than that seen in the past, making corresponding adjustments in attitudes that much more difficult. In an article written by Kilgour on the online catalog revolution, the author notes the strength of this "precedent-shattering socio-technological change."[4] The malady of library anxiety has been known to exist for quite some time prior to any appearance of computers in libraries. Mellon's study published in 1986 found that 75 to 85 percent of students in the study approached the library with fear.[5] Later articles written by Mellon in 1988,[6] Westbrook and DeDecker in 1993,[7] and Mark and Jacobson in 1995[8] provide suggestions for dealing with existence of this affliction, but it is a difficult state to overcome. The overall problem of library anxiety is made even worse by the overwhelming expansion of available information. With markedly increased feelings of insecurity and anxiety than experienced previously, the patron may be apt to develop even stronger feelings about their willingness to use particular formats prior to arriving inside the library.

SEARCHING BEHAVIOR AND ATTITUDES: RELATED RESEARCH ACCOMPLISHED

Various types of online resources have been in existence long enough now for a number of evaluative studies to have been conducted. Some of the first dealt with end-user use of online search utilities such as BRS and Dialog. Other studies have focused on the use of online public access catalogs and their impact on patron search behaviors, as well as their reactions to using OPACs as a means of access. Elements such as frustration, expectation, impact of memory, perseverance, and affability were explored in two studies done by Dalrymple published in 1990[9] and 1992,[10] with the results of the first, interesting enough, indicating that those searching for information in the card catalog retrieved more items and appeared more satisfied than those using an online public access catalog. On the contrary, a study done by York and others concluded that automation is very attractive, even to those who do not use library sources frequently.[11] A very recent study done by Snavely and Clark is useful for exploring some of the frustrations encountered by patrons specifically in finding serials via online public access catalogs.[12] Particularly interesting comments are noted in Chen's study of online catalog searching behavior of high school students, where the author indicates that earlier studies found less success in searching online catalogs at all age levels from elementary age to adults.[13] Some also question whether users are skilled in using any format of a catalog at all, card catalog or computerized.[14]

In research done by Hert, a newer model for dealing with human interactions with information retrieval systems and considerations for future research are discussed.[15] Studies such as those done by Wildemuth discussing student's misconceptions found in analysis of their search process,[16] by Tenopir and others of novices' searching experiences with the discovery of the "single-mindedness" of their search strategies,[17] and by Reneker regarding the information seeking patterns of those in the academic community[18] are particularly useful as well. Even gender may play a role, according to research done by Jacobson showing that males feel more comfortable using computers and computerized library materials, although females seem overall more comfortable with library settings.[19] All of such types of research will be useful in assisting in the development of computerized systems which take better into account the characteristics of how users search. The resulting systems hopefully will help combat the reluctance of some patrons to adopt the computerized resources.

Most of the studies already published have indicated the immense complexities of trying to measure behavior and attitudes of users of library resources, and a study done by Hancock-Beaulieu and others points out the further complication of determining user performance versus system performance, which are intimately intertwined.[20]

PATRONS WITH PRESET ATTITUDES
FOR USE OF PRINT MATERIALS

In an academic setting, those patrons with very limited knowledge of computers may show a very strong preference toward print resources. Understandably from the perspective of those users neither familiar nor proficient in computer search skills, it may seem too time-consuming to spend what extra time is needed to learn to use the computer software to search for citations or sources. Because they view the codex printed form as "easy" and the computerized equivalent "hard," they are reluctant to experiment with the latter. For some topics, either means of access would be equally productive. However, for a very detailed or specific query, multiple concept topic, or searching a new term not yet established as a descriptor term, for example, a computerized search may be far more productive depending on the software involved. In instances such as these, the patron who insists on use of a print index may never end up finding even a single related source and ends up assuming that there has been nothing written on the topic.

Proponents of print resources who decry the advent of computerized materials as inferior fail to recognize some of the drawbacks of print resources. The main library catalog, the most frequently used reference tool, is an excellent example, with some who are totally reluctant to withdraw from using the old standby of the card catalog purporting the strong merits of the old system over the newer computerized online public access catalogs. Some concerns are quite valid, such as complete lack of access when an online catalog is unavailable because of downtime.[21] What is overlooked is that the card catalog had more than its share of problems as well, with the patron perhaps missing access to some materials because of failure to understand the alphabetization system used (letter by letter versus word by word), failure to understand complex filing rules (sometimes so complex it was hard enough for librarians to decipher), human error in misfiling cards, and perhaps even a lack of understanding by the patron that the catalog was divided. In addition, space needs and costliness of card catalogs made them very expensive entities. Rider's article points out "the gravest single defect of the card catalog is that it is unitary" and goes on to describe it as "a bibliography in an edition of one copy."[22] Those who wish to remain solely with a print catalog fail to realize the tremendous and significant impact of the remote access capabilities of computerized catalogs.

It may be a long and difficult task for the librarian to convince patrons set on using only print sources of the positive aspects of online resources. Those with limited ability in the search process itself, coupled with little experience with computers, will of course be reluctant to take on those two new things simultaneously in their attempts to learn to use library sources. In the process of providing reference service, even if the reference librarian can convince a patron who is less familiar with the automated world to attempt a computerized search, it may be difficult to accomplish the level of instruction necessary the first few times, particularly if the patron approaches for assistance during a busy period of time. Progress will be painfully slow if the patron lacks a basic knowledge of keyboard skills. It is almost impossible to discuss at length the idea of a search strategy for a computerized index when, for instance, the patron is concentrating on finding where the number sign is located on the keyboard and how to produce the symbol. The patron may also display the attitude that it is not their responsibility to learn such basic keyboarding skills themselves, but part of the librarian's responsibility to show them as part of the instruction in use of the computerized resource. In most cases, the patron will likely leave the library with their original notions reinforced against computerized resources. As time progresses and students in public schools are exposed to computer skills at earlier ages, the lack of basic familiarity with computers will most likely become less and less of a problem, but in the meantime, the extreme gap between knowledge of some and that of others in computer skills remains a major problem for reference service.

PATRONS WITH PRESET ATTITUDES FOR USE OF COMPUTERIZED RESOURCES

Those patrons who view computerized resources very positively may pose the opposite problems in terms of their preset opinions and impact on reference assistance. In many cases, patrons have found computerized resources so much easier and faster to use that they may reject the use of print means of access altogether. The reference librarian may find that such patrons will refuse to use a print source perfectly tailored to their need in deference to a much less adequate computerized source because of their opinion that the automated source is always "better" (translation usually meaning faster). With increased teaching and other loads in recent years, not all faculty may have the time themselves to fully experiment with computerized resources and may therefore pass on impressions rather than direct knowledge of capabilities of particular computerized products, which may or may not be totally accurate, sometimes exacerbating the problem. With the high cost of access to online indexing sources and CD-ROM reference products, most libraries must make hard choices regarding what reference sources to provide in computerized form and what items to supply in print format, which at present is usually the less expensive option of the two. Amount of expected use, importance of currency of the content, and most important types of searching access needed will usually dictate the final choices selected, but patrons rarely will know or realize the impact of these decisions and may be very frustrated that a particular source is not available in a given library in computerized form. The cost of converting some materials to computerized form may be prohibitively expensive for the amount of projected future use, so the patron must be informed that not all items can be made available in computerized format, at least in the near future.

The user who has discovered remote access to online public access catalogs and other off-site computerized resources naturally is attracted to the strong advantages of such access. In addition, positive attitudes toward such catalogs stem from the expanded methods of searching provided by such databases over the limited types of searching points in the older predecessor, the card catalog.

Some patrons who are extremely comfortable using computers don't fully understand their searching methods and/or results and sometimes may not even realize that their search has not been as successful as it could be if a better search strategy and technique were used. A number of online public access catalogs and index tools are quite complex to use, but their appearance to the user is very deceptively easy. One example is the use of a keyword title search in a search engine that is sensitive to the exact order of every word in the title. Most systems provide explanations, but it would be the rare patron who would read such information word for word. The patron may assume that he or she has been successful if some or any citations are received by the way that they have searched, but may not realize that they have missed many or some of the most important citations by their search method if, for instance, they have not used controlled vocabulary where it would be important for a subject search. Their easy and perceived "success" retrieving anything at all reinforces their attitude that searching via computerized format of resource is best, and they may never realize what they have missed in their information seeking, unless they find a need to consult a librarian for some other reason. The varying quality and character of each search engine will also impact the precision and relevance of the results of a search, and the patron is frequently unaware of how much they have missed.

PERSPECTIVES ON INFORMATION SEEKING AND IMPACT ON REFERENCE SERVICE

Many computer-savvy patrons have never really learned the basic strengths and weaknesses of both computerized searching and searching of print resources. Unfortunately, many patrons don't seem to have the patience to listen to such explanations. Either the emphasis in today's society on instant gratification, or increased demands and pressures of contemporary life (or perhaps a combination of both) lead most information seekers in the direction of their perceived fastest and easiest route to meet their information need. As the reference librarian works with each patron, he or she will have to try to convey the sense that the format of information sources in itself is not the primary concern, but rather the age-old process of effectively formulating the information question. A fast pace to obtain information can frequently obscure the need to reflect carefully on the basics of determining what it is that one actually wants and is searching for, even in the patron's own mind, as well as the important process of formulating the question in a comprehensible manner to the reference librarian. The ability to define the topic properly, including the aspects of deciding what it is that one wants and doesn't want, is just as important as it always was, but it is easy for the information seeker to lose sight of the primacy of framing the search question in the confusion over the variety and number of choices for finding information today. Patrons may also be unaware that narrowing or broadening their topic is still necessary even with computerized searching. It is very easy to become caught up in the pure mechanics of computer operation and/or the excitement of higher tech means of access, to the exclusion of the important concepts of the search and research process.

The recent nation-wide emphasis on information literacy points out this need to re-address the teaching of basic aspects of formulating the topic, as well as other essential elements of the research process, such as evaluation of materials obtained for the information need. The information explosion has escalated so fast and furiously that emphasis on such evaluation is sometimes forgotten. The American Association of School Librarians points out in their recent position statement the importance of information literacy in coping with the expected continuation of rapid change in today's world and the future. The same position statement contains an excellent outline of information problem-solving skills which are very relevant for many age levels, including students in higher education.[23] It seems a logical progression from the exploration of the concepts of information literacy that content of a resource is far more important than the format, print or computerized, of the source.

To help emphasize the evaluation process, the reference librarian needs to remind patrons during the course of their interaction that their goal isn't necessarily to just "find something" on their topic (although for an extremely narrow topic, of course, that may have to suffice), but to find the best information or sources on the topic, taking the time to determine how well the material is written, the author's or authors' experience or authority in that particular topic, and even whether the material actually answers their posed question, or just vaguely relates to the information need. Too often the patron is so muddled from all that is available, learning how to use so many new sources, and the total complexity of it all, that once they have retrieved possible materials, they fail to examine them carefully to discover that they don't really deal with the particular aspect of the topic for their information need. Determining what one has is complicated by the sheer mass of information available (as Blandy and Libutti put it, "like wind and waves, the information keeps flowing by") and the total mixture of levels of quality seen everywhere–"the coarse, the foolish, the unreliable, the malevolent, the beautiful, and the useful are all mixed up together in conversation, on the Internet, in magazines, on television."[24]

One of the hardest parts of today's reference service may be determining the patron's level of understanding and how much can be absorbed in any given interaction. Obvious preset attitudes may complicate the matter and mask the true situation. With varying levels of computer knowledge and expertise, the job becomes much more difficult for the librarian and is apt to remain a more severe problem until a basic level of computer literacy becomes the standard. For the patron fearful of computerized resources, who also lacks a good understanding of a search process using any format, the librarian may find the best approach to be a simpler explanation of a search in a print source, even when that particular resource may not be nearly as good as a computerized tool available, until the patron has some initial ease solely with the search process itself. Even if a reluctant patron can be successfully introduced to a computerized source, stronger features of the search engine, such as use of Boolean terms and truncation, may have to be excluded from instruction until the patron has had an opportunity to absorb the more basic searching concepts involved in computerized searching. No matter what the level the patron is at and what format type they seem to prefer, librarians need to be very careful not to "snow" the patron with too much complexity. As computerized search techniques and jargon terms become part of everyday life for librarians, it is easy to forget that what is taken for granted as basic to everyone's knowledge may not be to some.

Instruction via formal classes coupled with one-to-one instruction at the point of reference service in terms of the techniques and conceptual processes behind both types of searching, print and computerized, might help make at least small advances in combating the preconceptions about source formats. Most importantly, the need for flexibility and versatility will need to be emphasized as well, as today's patrons will need to be able to switch easily between print and computerized versions of even the same resource depending on which library's doors they walk through from one day to the next. Comfort with both formats will need to be developed for ease at least in the short-term, if not the long-term also. It is clear that the availability and use of computerized resources will continue to escalate, particularly as costs allow more smaller libraries to obtain access. Their importance is clearly recognized, and in fact, Force, in a recent article, proposes "online services offer the best possibility of bringing rich information resources to the most remote and poorest parts of the country."[25] However, the patron will also need to be able to use and value print materials. Hopkins, in his exploration of coping with information overload, indicates that a combination of both types of formats will be needed and comments, "Published guides, research handbooks and state-of-the-art review publications, for example, will undoubtedly continue to be important."[26] He goes on to point out that those wanting in-depth understanding of a subject area will probably choose to use these sources in print format, while those who wish to "focus quickly on the key sources of information in an area of knowledge"[27] will select these same materials in computerized format.

In working with those not yet computer literate, it is wise to take heed of Kay's suggestion to avoid a focus on teaching solely the technical in terms of the computer, which he terms as the "carrier," and his warning that the computer must be viewed as a vehicle only, not an end in itself.[28] Similar to this concern is Sheingold's statement that "past technologies have been promoted as 'the answer' for education" and the importance of "understanding that it is not the features of the technology alone, but rather the ways in which those features are used in human environments, that shape its impact."[29]

The process of helping students feel comfortable with the most important print and computerized resources will clearly require the participation of faculty in their course instruction as well. In an article written by Egan, the author goes as far as to propose that faculty themselves go to the library for required conferences with their students to introduce them to major resources in the particular subject area as part of their courses.[30] In terms of this process, both faculty and librarians will acquire new roles[31] and require new training.[32] A study done by Sievert and others indicates library staff themselves experience anxiety related to computers and technology.[33] It is clear that faculty and librarians will need to be more comfortable in their new roles and develop enough facility themselves with all formats in order to aid students in overcoming their reluctance to approach particular formats.

CONCLUSION

Overcoming patrons' preconceived notions of format and creating a balanced approach among all the information formats will take a long time to accomplish and, most likely, only partial success will ever be realized. A return to a stronger emphasis on the importance of material content, no matter how it is obtained, may have a strong impact on overcoming patrons' preconceived attitudes regarding types of resources. It must somehow be conveyed to the information seeker that underlying critical thinking and learning skills will be the means of adjusting to all the future massive changes in information access and that rapid changes will now be the expected norm in today's world as part of everyday life.

REFERENCES

1. Richard L. Hopkins, "Countering Information Overload: The Role of the Librarian," *Reference Librarian* 49/50(1995): 305-333.
2. Michael Stuart Freeman, "Pen, Ink, Keys, and Cards: Some Reflections on Library Technology," *College & Research Libraries* 52(July 1991): 328-35.
3. Susan Griswold Blandy and Patricia O'Brien Libutti, "As the Cursor Blinks: Electronic Scholarship and Undergraduates in the Library," *Library Trends* 44(Fall 1995): 279-305.
4. Frederick G. Kilgour, "The Online Catalog Revolution," *Library Journal* 109(February 15, 1984): 320.
5. Constance A. Mellon, "Library Anxiety: A Grounded Theory and Its Development," *College & Research Libraries* 47(March 1986): 160-165.
6. Constance A. Mellon, "Attitudes: The Forgotten Dimension in Library Instruction," *Library Journal* 113(September 1, 1988): 137-39.
7. Lynn Westbrook and Sharon DeDecker, "Supporting User Needs and Skills to Minimize Library Anxiety: Considerations for Academic Libraries," *Reference Librarian* 40(1993): 43-51.
8. Beth L. Mark and Trudi E. Jacobson, "Teaching Anxious Students Skills for the Electronic Library," *College Teaching* 43(Winter 1995): 28-31.
9. Prudence W. Dalrymple, "Retrieval by Reformulation in Two Library Catalogs: Toward a Cognitive Model of Searching Behavior," *Journal of the American Society for Information Science* 41(June 1990): 272-81.
10. Prudence W. Dalrymple, "Users' Experience of Information Retrieval Systems: An Exploration of the Relationship Between Search Experience and Affective Measures," *Library and Information Science Research* 14(June 1992): 167-81.
11. Charlene C. York and others, "Computerized Reference Sources: One-Stop Shopping or Part of a Search Strategy?" *Research Strategies* 6(Winter 1988): 8-17.
12. Loanne Snavely and Katie Clark, "What Users Really Think: How They See and Find Serials in the Arts and Sciences," *Library Resources & Technical Services* 40(January 1996): 49-60.
13. Shu-Hsien Chen, "A Study of High School Students' Online Catalog Searching Behavior," *School Library Media Quarterly* 22(Fall 1993): 33-40.
14. David R. McDonald and Susan E. Searing, "Bibliographic Instruction and the Development of Online Catalogs," *College & Research Libraries* 44(January 1983): 5-11.
15. Carol A. Hert, "Exploring a New Model for Understanding Information Retrieval Interactions," *Proceedings of the ASIS Annual Meeting* 29(1992): 72-75.

16. Barbara M. Wildemuth, "Post-Positivist Research: Two Examples of Methodological Pluralism," *Library Quarterly* 63(October 1993): 450-68.

17. Carol Tenopir, Diane Nahl-Jakobovits, and Dara Lee Howard, "Strategies and Assessments Online: Novices' Experience," *Library & Information Science Research* 13(July/September 1991): 237-66.

18. Maxine H. Reneker, "A Qualitative Study of Information Seeking Among Members of an Academic Community: Methodological Issues and Problems," *Library Quarterly* 63(October 1993): 487-507.

19. Frances F. Jacobson, "Gender Differences in Attitudes Toward Using Computers in Libraries: An Exploratory Study," *Library & Information Science Research* 13(September 1991): 267-79.

20. Micheline Hancock-Beaulieu, Stephen Robertson, and Colin Neilson, "Evaluation of Online Catalogues: Eliciting Information From the User," *Information Processing & Management* 27(1991): 523-32.

21. Carol Walton, Susan Williamson, and Howard D. White, "Resistance to Online Catalogs: A Comparative Study at Bryn Mawr and Swarthmore Colleges," *Library Resources & Technical Services* 30(October/December 1986): 388-401.

22. Fremont Rider, "The Possibility of Discarding the Card Catalog," *Library Quarterly* 8(July 1938): 330.

23. American Association of School Librarians, "Information Literacy: A Position Paper on Information Problem Solving," *Emergency Librarian* 23(November/December 1995): 20-23.

24. Blandy, 284.

25. Ron Force, "Planning Online Reference Services for the 90s," *Reference Librarian* 43(1994): 114.

26. Hopkins, 330.

27. Ibid.

28. Alan C. Kay, "Computers, Networks and Education," *Scientific American* 265(September 1991): 138-48.

29. Karen Sheingold, "Restructuring for Learning With Technology: The Potential for Synergy," *Phi Delta Kappan* 73(September 1991): 18.

30. Philip J. Egan, "Bridging the Gap Between the Student and the Library," *College Teaching* 40(1992): 67-70.

31. Kenneth C. Green and Steven W. Gilbert, "Content, Communications, Productivity, and the Role of Information Technology in Higher Education," *Change* 27(March/April 1995): 8-18; Thomas Klein, "Electronic Revolution at the Educational Crossroads: Foot-Dragging On Campus," *College Teaching* 43(Fall 1995): 151-55.

32. Hong Xu, "The Impact of Automation on Job Requirements and Qualifications for Catalogers and Reference Librarians in Academic Libraries," *Library Resources & Technical Services* 40(January 1996): 9-31.

33. MaryEllen Sievert and others, "Investigating Computer Anxiety in an Academic Library," *Information Technology and Libraries* 7(September 1988): 243-52.

Index

Access issues, for Geographic
  Information Systems,
  101-107
Advanced Research Projects Agency,
  96
Advertising, metaphors in, 53
Affective domain in information
  seeking, 12,14
Alta Vista
  co-citation mapping, 58
  evaluation, 30-43
  simulation of search tactics of
    Web users, 66-68,70
Analytical models, 7-8
Anxiety of patrons, 129
ArcView, 95-96,98-99,104-107
Arizona, University of, 57,96,99
Articulated cognitive style, 11
Association of Research Libraries
  GIS Literacy Project, 95-96
Attribute data in Geographic
  Information Systems, 90,
  95,104-107
Author search on Internet, 68-69

Browsers, types of, 63,71
Budget. *See* Financial issues

Card catalogs, 129-131
Cartographic Users Advisory
  Council, 95
Catholic University of America,
  64-81
CD-ROMs, 96
Census Bureau, 94-95
Census files in GIS, 95

Clearinghouse of Subject-Oriented
  Internet Resources, 28
Co-citation mapping, 57-59
Cognitive processes
  defined, 4-5
  maps in aiding, 54
  models of users, 7-14
  in use of information systems, 5-6
Cognitive styles
  defined, 6
  in search performance, 11-12
Cognitive walkthrough, 20
Collaborations, 100,124
Competing values approach, 111-126
  current state of reference
    management, 113-115
  framework, 116-121
  implications, 123-125
  vs. other models, 122-123
  trends in reference service,
    112-113
Conceptual models, 7
Connecticut, University of, 97,99
Cornell University, 96-97
Corporate body search on Internet,
  68-69,71,78-79
Corporations, 88
Cranfield studies, 9
Cultural issues in visualization of
  information, 53-54

Data analysis
  search engine retrieval power, 33
  simulation of search tactics of
    Web users, 66-67
Databases. *See also* Geographic
  Information Systems

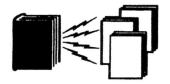

Haworth
DOCUMENT DELIVERY
SERVICE

This valuable service provides a single-article order form for any article from a Haworth journal.

- *Time Saving:* No running around from library to library to find a specific article.
- *Cost Effective:* All costs are kept down to a minimum.
- *Fast Delivery:* Choose from several options, including same-day FAX.
- *No Copyright Hassles:* You will be supplied by the original publisher.
- *Easy Payment:* Choose from several easy payment methods.

> ***Open Accounts Welcome for . . .***
> - Library Interlibrary Loan Departments
> - Library Network/Consortia Wishing to Provide Single-Article Services
> - Indexing/Abstracting Services with Single Article Provision Services
> - Document Provision Brokers and Freelance Information Service Providers

MAIL or *FAX* THIS ENTIRE ORDER FORM TO:

Haworth Document Delivery Service	**or FAX:** 1-800-895-0582
The Haworth Press, Inc.	**or CALL:** 1-800-342-9678
10 Alice Street	9am-5pm EST
Binghamton, NY 13904-1580	

PLEASE SEND ME PHOTOCOPIES OF THE FOLLOWING SINGLE ARTICLES:

1) Journal Title: _____
    Vol/Issue/Year:_____Starting & Ending Pages:_____
    Article Title:_____

2) Journal Title: _____
    Vol/Issue/Year:_____Starting & Ending Pages:_____
    Article Title:_____

3) Journal Title: _____
    Vol/Issue/Year:_____Starting & Ending Pages:_____
    Article Title:_____

4) Journal Title: _____
    Vol/Issue/Year:_____Starting & Ending Pages:_____
    Article Title:_____

(See other side for Costs and Payment Information)

COSTS: Please figure your cost to order quality copies of an article.

1. Set-up charge per article: $8.00
   ($8.00 × number of separate articles) _____

2. Photocopying charge for each article:
   1-10 pages: $1.00 _____

   11-19 pages: $3.00 _____

   20-29 pages: $5.00 _____

   30+ pages: $2.00/10 pages _____

3. Flexicover (optional): $2.00/article _____

4. Postage & Handling: US: $1.00 for the first article/
   $.50 each additional article _____

   Federal Express: $25.00 _____

   Outside US: $2.00 for first article/
   $.50 each additional article_____

5. Same-day FAX service: $.35 per page _____

GRAND TOTAL: _____

METHOD OF PAYMENT: (please check one)
❑ Check enclosed   ❑ Please ship and bill. PO # _____
(sorry we can ship and bill to bookstores only! All others must pre-pay)

❑ Charge to my credit card: ❑ Visa; ❑ MasterCard; ❑ Discover;
❑ American Express;

Account Number:_____ Expiration date:_____

Signature: ✗_____

Name: _____ Institution: _____

Address: _____

_____

City: _____ State:_____ Zip:_____

Phone Number: _____ FAX Number: _____

MAIL or *FAX* THIS ENTIRE ORDER FORM TO:

Haworth Document Delivery Service	**or FAX:** 1-800-895-0582
The Haworth Press, Inc.	**or CALL:** 1-800-342-9678
10 Alice Street	9am-5pm EST)
Binghamton, NY 13904-1580	